SOME WERE LUCKY

For May
With love &
best wishes

Eric Goodwin
9th August 1997

SOME WERE LUCKY

by

Eric Goodwin

Published by

Eric Goodwin
22 Wentworth Gate
WETHERBY
LS22 6XD

Copyright © 1996, 1997 Eric Goodwin

All rights reserved. No part of this publication may be reproduced, stored in a retrieval system, or transmitted in any form or by any means, electronic, mechanical, photocopying, recording or otherwise, without prior permission in writing from Eric Goodwin.

Eric Goodwin has asserted his moral right to be identified as the author of this work.

ISBN 0 9530124 0 9
Produced by
Axxent Ltd
The Old Council Offices, The Green
Datchet, Berkshire
SL3 9EH

Eric and Marjorie 1994

PREFACE

This account is a true reflection on my character, insofar that it develops and ends in a far different way than originally intended.

Meant to be my "memoirs," the story of my life for the benefit and boredom of my surviving family, after a promising start in that direction it reaches the war period and there it firmly stays.

Three years after leaving school I was transported into a different world, where, because life was cheap, it was valued all the more highly. The warmth and companionship of the friends I made during those years of conflict, many of whom were killed, remain with me to this day. At the time it happened those of us who lived on either developed a hardened attitude to life, or went under. Some of us were lucky.............others were not.

Over fifty years have now gone by since then. Memories of so long ago do not dim with age, if anything they grow even more vivid. It is only today, and the coming of a brief tomorrow that become shrouded in the mists of time.

I have endeavoured to tell the truth of events as they happened, and not to exaggerate – rather the opposite. I have omitted any reference to flying, airborne and Air Sea Rescue incidents which cannot be substantiated by RAF Records.

The fact that anything has been written at all is entirely the fault of my second wife, Marjorie, and my good friends Peter Clarke and Rob Ward who refuse to allow me to doze idly in my armchair when they have to go out to work.

If you enjoy reading this, thank them, not me.

CHAPTER 1

A Twig off the Branch

There is nothing in my family history which indicates that I was destined to distinguish myself in any form of military fame. Time was to prove this to be true, as my story will show. Like all the others of my generation war was a school history subject, not something which would ever happen in our lifetime and in which we would be involved.

Yet we were – and many of us were to die. Some were lucky, I was one of them.

That was a long time ago and I can now look back on those days remembering, as is human nature, more of the good days than the others.

A long time ago..................
So that is where I'll begin.

The name Goodwin is common enough in England perhaps proving that, going back into the mists of time, it may well have historic connections. Whether those would be something to be proud of maybe it is as well we do not know. One dubious claim to fame is that one of our earlier ancestors, famous for losing an "I" to an arrow also lost an "O" from his name, became known as Godwin, and was an English king. A keen sportsman, he lost a home match against the Normans in 1066, ever since then his descendants have usually had to work for their living.

I never knew my own grandparents. They all died at comparatively young ages in the 1880's and 1890's. My particular branch of the Goodwins originated from Yorkshire, in the Hull area, and my father's father was a painter and decorator.

Mother's maiden name was Knowles, her father being a well-known publican in the Portwood district of Stockport in the latter half of the nineteenth century. Her mother was Irish from a family called O'Divers who came to this country from Southern Ireland about 1860. Family legend says that her parents managed a public house in the area known as Tiviot Dale called the "Crown and Mitre", more commonly referred to by the regular customers as the "Crown Almighty". Here my maternal grandfather met a spectacular death when a landslip took the outside privy in which he was meditating down the bank into the River Tame, a tributary of the Mersey, which happened to be in full spate. He and his wife, originally interred in one of the local churchyards now lie, with many others, underneath a large roundabout on the area's road development scheme.

Christened Mary Elizabeth Knowles, mother was born on the 23rd of October 1890. She was seven years younger than my father, Stephen, who was born in 1883 on February 6th (the same date as my own birthday). Both my parents were christened Roman Catholic. By a strange coincidence the two were orphaned whilst babies and adopted by Protestant families.

In the case of my father this was by a family named Ford, who lived in Sidney Street, Offerton, Stockport. They were great folk. The son of mother Ford, Joe, had a good job at Battersby's hat works and was greatly respected. In fact he was looked upon with some awe as he had been sent by his employer to the USA. A real adventure in the early 1900's when the only way to get there was to go by sea. Joe had two sisters, the eldest, Nellie, wed and had one son. Her married name was Williamson. The younger sister, Liza, remained a spinster all her life. She was a sweet and gentle person and my favourite aunt. I cannot be sure but I think her one and only boy friend was killed in either the Boer War or World War One. As did Nellie, Liza lived to be in her nineties.

When they were very young, and before they were adopted, both my mother and father were cared for by the

Pendlebury Orphanage, which was on Dodge Hill, the old Roman road which climbs up to Heaton Norris from the bottom of Lancashire Hill. However, they met for the first time about 1906 when they were members of the choir at the Union Chapel. This place of worship stood at the junction of Hall Street and Banks Lane but was demolished about 1980. They were married here in 1910 which, if my arithmetic is correct means that my mother would be 20 and father 27.

In her maiden name of Elizabeth Knowles my mother was well-known as a very talented singer. She had an unusually rich alto voice and was offered an appointment with the Doyle Carte Opera Company. Being newly married she declined. She had two brothers, George and Alfred, who were a little older than herself, I think. During the First World War George failed the medical examination for the Forces and was sent to work in the shipyards of Tyneside. Alf became a sergeant in the Cheshire Regiment and spent three years in the trench warfare in France. After the war George became a coal merchant and Alf resident storekeeper at what was then known as the Stockport Electricity Works. Both married but only Alf's first wife, Annie, produced any children, Kenneth, Winifred and Frank. They have all been dead for many years and his second wife, Ida died in July 1992.

My father, Stephen, had a brother Jack who, after retiring from his trade as a confectioner resided at Marple. He had three children, Ivy, Lorna and Jack who, following an adventurous early life ended his career as a signalman on the now defunct railway line at Higher Poynton. As well as a brother my father had two sisters Maude and Bessie. Maude married a solicitor and had a daughter, Hilda. Their home was in the Woodsmoor district of Stockport and they died a long time ago. The other sister, Bessie, married a man called Coppin. He was always in trouble with the Stockport police and had the reputation of being violent. What happened to him I never knew, but Bessie moved to Blackpool and had quite a successful career. I last met her when training there with the RAF in 1940. She was Manageress of the Palace bar and kind enough to treat her poor airman nephew to a drink whenever he called in to see her. Bessie had two daughters (whose names I can't remember) and a son. I think he was called Wilf and I understand he played for Arsenal in the 1930's as a halfback and was capped for England.

When my parents were married Stockport was renowned for the production and distribution of men's hats. Father worked as a "Hatter's Warehouseman" for one of the town's leading companies Ward Brothers. The last time I was in the town the old Ward Brothers building was still there. It is the tall mill-like structure on Wellington Road South overlooking where the buses used to be parked off Mersey Square. The letter "W" for Ward could still be seen at the very top.

Apart from her musical engagements I do not know what Mother did in the early days of their married life. They lived in one of the terraced houses on Dialstone Lane opposite what was then the Battersby Social Club and is now the Belgrade Hotel.

In 1914 came the First World War. Being 31 years old it appeared unlikely that my father would be called up, but the carnage of that conflict meant men up to the age of 40 would be conscripted into the fighting services. It was 1916 when Dad joined the Royal Welch Fusiliers (yes – the spelling is correct) and within a few weeks was in the front line in France. As a boy the stories I used to hear from him and others about the horrors of Ypres and Paschendale were to influence me years later.

Poison gas was used extensively in that war and my father was one of those affected by it. As a result he got a small army pension. When he died, aged 77, there had to be an autopsy to establish that his war injuries had not contributed to his death!

Whilst her husband was in the army Mother did night work at a munitions factory located in Georges Road, which is located on the left-hand side of Wellington Road North as you climb out of Mersey Square en route to Manchester. In 1916, or 1917, there was an air raid alert when a German Zeppelin wandered somewhere over the Buxton area eighteen miles away. Work in the factory was suspended. To keep up the morale of the women operators Mother organised a singsong. This was quickly quelled by an irate overseer with the immortal words : "Quiet you silly bitches, the Huns will hear you!"

Demobbed in 1919 Dad went back to Ward Brothers and Mother became pregnant. The result was my appearance on February 6th 1920. Four years later on February 1st 1924 my brother Alan was born. Unfortunately he only lived six months, dying of a condition which would today be easily corrected. He is buried in the Locke family grave in Stockport cemetery.

Mrs Locke, Auntie Polly, belonged to another branch of the family, as also did the loveable old couple I knew as Uncle Alf and Aunty Sally Wyche. They lived in Parsonage Street, Heaton Norris and had two daughters Sarah-Anne and Marie. Well in to her seventies Aunt Sally had sparkling white teeth, which I was assured was entirely due to assiduously cleaning them every day with a mixture of soot and water. I tried it once and was soundly scolded for making an unholy mess of my clothes and kitchen.

Christmas Eve always brings back to me vibrant memories of those times. When a young boy I would be sent to bed in the afternoon in the mistaken belief that I would have two or three hours sleep to fortify me for the night's festivities. That never occurred, I was always too excited to even doze. Father would come home from work about six o'clock and, having changed in to his best suit we would set off on the walk of two miles from our house to Aunt Sally's.

There the table would be laden with home-made Christmas cake, mince pies, sausage rolls and fancy cakes. From the cramped kitchen, then known as the scullery, – but illuminated with the most up-to-date gas mantle – came the appetising aroma of rabbit pie. This would be served about ten o'clock with great pomp and ceremony, together with a glass of port wine. The climax of the night came when Uncle Alf arrived home from his club where he had been for the previous three or four hours. White moustache somewhat bedraggled, but bowler hat planted firmly on his head, he would wish us all a Merry Christmas, ask for the blessing of God on Santa Claus and Queen Victoria (who had been dead for many years), have a drink from a bottle of whisky which he would produce from the depths of his overcoat, and sit down at the piano. Unerringly his fingers struck the right chord and the assembled company lustily burst forth into what was the annual family anthem. The only words I can remember, and actually knew at the time, were "The mighty mountains echo." This was repeated over, and over again, the word "echo" constantly repeated and reverberating with increased volume. The climax of the night came when Fanny and Oswald (two other far-flung relatives) came in about 1am after attending a Midnight Mass service. With Uncle Alf, bowler hat still worn with dignity, accompanying them on the piano, they launched into their off-key version of "Oh, come all ye faithful." This was rendered in what my father said was a conglomeration of the Cheshire Chant and Lancashire Latin – although we all knew the tune we didn't understand a word they were singing.

This wonderful night ended with the walk back to our home. I always recall the sharp, clear, frosty weather, the chiming of two o'clock by St Mary's church in the market place, and my anxious scanning of the sky for Santa and his reindeer. I desperately hoped that he would not call at our house before we arrived, find it empty, and not leave any presents. Luckily he always did.

In 1924 I began my education at Banks Lane school. This building was demolished about 1987. At the age of eleven I won what was then known as a scholarship which meant a transfer to Stockport Secondary School on Greek Street. The front entrance was on Wellington Road South, but this has also changed tremendously since 1980. The Secondary School was relocated and renamed Stockport School at Mile End Lane in 1938. My mother was in charge of the kitchen, preparing meals for pupils and staff, and worked there until her death in 1954.

A Twig off the Branch

Leaving school in 1936, without achieving any notable academic success, I joined the London Midland Railway my first appointment being to Poynton station, in those days an excellent training ground as it handled both goods and passenger traffic. The Station Master, named Heyworth, lived with his wife and daughter in the house provided on the station drive. The daughter, Vera, was an attractive girl of my own age, but my clumsy attempts at flirting were always thwarted by her strict father. Another local sixteen year old beauty was Mary. Her father was Alan Shatwell, the area coal agent, who played hell if we didn't get his rail wagons into the sidings on time. I was far too afraid of him to make any amorous approaches to Mary. In those days most goods and parcels came by rail and deliveries were done on a contract basis by a private haulier Bert Hallworth. When I first went to the station the gasworks had just closed but the branch line which went past it down to Poynton Collieries (later Lancashire Coal) was still open, a level crossing took it across the main Macclesfield – Stockport road and up through the woods to the other line at Higher Poynton.

There was a two shift system of working for the clerks at Poynton station, 7 am – 3 pm and 2 pm – 10 pm. I was on the late turn one evening when, at about eight o'clock there was a timid knock on the grille of the booking office. Her name was Nora, an extremely attractive seventeen-year old blonde girl who wanted to know if her friend, Ivy Hopkinson, had arrived some thirty minutes before on the train from Stockport. Looking back I have often wondered if this was just an excuse to see what I looked like. However, she was a lovely girl and from that night I had eyes for no one else.

Working shifts on the railway meant that Nora and I could only go out together every other week. Our courting consisted of walks round Poynton Pool, Towers Road, the Coppice, Higher Poynton and Middlewood. Occasionally we would go to Hope Green where, in those days her father, Jim Mountfort, had a farm.

A special treat was going to the Brookfield cinema on a Saturday night. I had to wear my best suit for this which meant I could not ride my bike. The best seats cost one shilling and sixpence (about 7½ pence in the money of today). My parents allowed me to keep four shillings (20p) out of my weekly wage of £1. I usually walked the five miles from my home in Stockport to Poynton on those nights, and later five miles back again, otherwise I could not afford to buy my girl friend an ice cream.

In late 1937, with the war clouds gathering, the British Government introduced conscription for all men as they attained the age of eighteen. Remembering the stories of the horrific experiences suffered in the army by my father and his friends during the previous conflict, I initially endeavoured to join the air crew training scheme for the newly-forming Fleet Air Arm. My academic qualifications were not good enough. Lucky me, if I had been accepted I would most likely have finished up on the antiquated Swordfish aircraft – and I do mean finished! Still determined to avoid the army I then volunteered for aircrew duties with the RAF. At that point of time only men with a university education had the opportunity to be trained as pilots or navigators. Later on a casualty rate of 80% inevitably changed this policy. My own education qualified me for training as a Wireless Operator/Air Gunner, and as such I joined the RAF Volunteer Reserve. However, the country was ill-prepared for war and there were neither sufficient training facilities nor aircraft for us to fly. The conflict would be almost a year old before I, and many others like me, would be called up to the armed forces.

CHAPTER 2

Getting Ready

Compared to many I suppose "my War" could be called interesting insofar that initially a member of a bomber crew, I was next attached to the 1st Airborne Division and then experienced some months on an Air Sea Rescue launch. I was stationed at UK bases as far apart as Cornwall, northern Scotland and the Western Isles and saw a little of the world when in Algeria, Tunisia and India.

I was also involved in the invasions of French Northern Africa, Sicily and the D-Day landings. Quite a varied diet, all the more remarkable as, apart from in the beginning, expressing a desire to be aircrew, I volunteered for none of it! Memories of those times still remain, especially those of the friends I made and lost. It was really the old, old story of life, some were lucky, and I was one of them ....others were not.

The war began on September 3rd, 1939, at eleven o'clock in the morning. Immediately after the radio announcement I went to the 'phone box by the main gates of nearby Woodbank Park to speak to Nora. We arranged to meet in Poynton that evening. Outside her mother's shop at 39 London Road South we listened, together with her sister Nellie and husband Jack Rothwell, to the news on his car radio. By today's standards that radio was a monstrous affair with valves and wires all over the place – the transistor had not then been invented. Roy, Nora's brother was there too, he was eleven years old at the time.

In 1938 I had been transferred from Poynton station to Cheadle Heath, Stockport. Still working shifts Nora and I went out together when I was on the early turn, and sometimes she would travel on the bus to Stockport to spend a few minutes with me before I caught the tramcar from Mersey Square to Cheadle Heath when I was working on the late shift from three o'clock in the afternoon until eleven in the evening. After the war began, returning home at that time on my bicycle in the blackout with only the faint glimmer of a restricted headlight was possibly as perilous as anything else I was later to experience. The only other assistance to road-users were the white bands painted round the bottom of roadside trees. One blessing was that there was little, or no, motor traffic. In addition to the perils of the blackout there was strict petrol rationing and, of course, there were far fewer cars on the road than today.

For many months the war made very little difference to our lives. The blackout was an inconvenience suffered by everyone. The Germans and the Allies seemed to be content sitting looking at each other from their respective fortifications. The sirens occasionally wailed an air raid alert, usually about 2 am, when mother would insist we all get out of bed and out into the cold, damp Anderson shelter Dad had installed in the back garden. The uneven drone of an enemy bomber, sometimes accompanied by a photographic parachute flare, was all that ever happened. Like others of my age I was anxious to be in the services before the war finished. Two letters I wrote to the RAF pleading for some action were answered by brief notes telling me to be patient – my time would come. Ah, the innocence of youth!

It was, in August 1940 that instructions finally came for me to report at Padgate, near Warrington, for initial training. Six week's "square bashing" there was followed by a four months course in Morse and radio procedures at the Winter Gardens, Blackpool. Most weekends, I managed to get back home to my parents and Nora. Official leave passes were few and far between and it was a battle of wits between the RAF Service Police and several hundred recalcitrant airmen to, first of all, get out of the town and the following night get back in again.

Getting Ready

Getting out was comparatively easy, there were so many roads where with patience, and a bit of luck airmen could hitch a lift from some sympathetic driver. Coming back was a different matter. As everyone left the time of their return as late as possible the early morning mail train from Manchester was the favourite method. There were hundreds of us on this, I don't know how many paid their fare – I never did. The train stopped at the small station of Blackpool South about four in the morning before terminating at Central. It was always a question of guessing at which station most of the S.P.'s would be lining the platform as to where we disgorged from the train. If we guessed right we would greatly outnumber the unfortunate upholders of the law and a mad rush breaking through their ranks would take us to safety and back to the anonymity of our billets for a couple of hours sleep before reveille. Only once was I with a crowd which guessed wrongly. Getting off at a seemly deserted Blackpool station we were surprised by a rush of S.P.'s from the other side of the tracks. In the chaos and consternation which followed I found myself at the rear of the fleeing mob. To my horror two burly policemen singled me out for arrest and a hectic chase followed for the next twenty minutes or so. I finished up panting and exhausted near an ornamental lake which, I learned later, was in Stanley Park, miles from the station. There was no sleep for me that night, by the time I had crept furtively through the now deserted streets it was time for roll call.

The visit home which I remember most was at Christmas time, December 1940. After Sunday tea with my mother and father at their house in Forbes Road, Stockport, Nora and I left at about six o'clock so that she could catch a bus to Poynton before I went on to Manchester where I would get a train to Blackpool. As we left the air raid sirens wailed their warning and within minutes German bombers were droning overhead. Anti-aircraft fire added to the din and falling shrapnel from exploding shells began to clang and spark off the road surface. The night sky flared and flickered as incendiaries took hold of the buildings in Manchester city centre and the crump of high explosive bombs became ever more frequent and closer.

It became obvious there would be no bus services that night!

The best possible action that there appeared to be was to walk to the Edgeley railway station, put Nora on a train to her home village of Poynton, and I would go in the opposite direction on a train to Manchester.

There were no trains going anywhere.

At least the telephones were working and I was able to speak to Jack Rothwell and ask for help. With great courage he drove to the station, where Nora and I were sheltering in the subway. Jack took Nora to Poynton and I walked back to my parent's house to find them, together with their next-door neighbours huddled under a table in the lounge. There certainly was no room there for anyone else! Resisting entreaties from Mother to go and take refuge and sit in the cold, damp garden air raid shelter I made myself a cup of tea and, despite the racket going on outside managed to doze fitfully until the sirens sounded the "All Clear." This was the first air raid I had experienced and, at that time I felt no fear, the main concentration of the bombing was some six miles away. Sometime later it was to be much closer, after that my stomach churned over with terror as soon as the sirens started their mournful wail.

The next morning I had to walk from Stockport to Manchester where bomb-blasted buildings were still burning. Trains were running from Victoria, although the adjacent Exchange station appeared badly damaged. Rumour had it that a Heinkel bomber had crashed down through the roof. Whatever it was it looked a smoking ruin.

I was late in reporting back to my unit, but luckily I had been on official leave – so I received sympathy, not punishment.

After Blackpool further training followed at Yatesbury in Wiltshire. Here I flew for the first time, in a twin-engined plane – a De Havilland Dominie. There were usually six trainee wireless operators together with the pilot in the twin-engined biplane. We had to take turns in using the aircraft's radio equipment as the pilot took us in lazy circles above Wiltshire and occasionally the city of Bath.

Getting Ready

By March 1941 I had been taught the rudiments of radio communication and maintenance but the air gunnery schools were still not able to cope with the rapidly expanding numbers of aircrew. Consequently I was posted as a ground operator to Mountbatten, Plymouth, a small promontory in Plymouth Sound which was the base of an Australian squadron of Sunderland flying boats. Billeted on the base in what, pre-war, had been the married quarters, life was pleasant enough – at first. There were four airmen occupying each house and I shared a room with Jackie Bennett, my own age, small of stature but with a big heart and full of fun. We worked round the twenty-four hours shifts in the operations room, an underground concrete bunker which, we were assured, was bomb-proof. The headquarters of 19 Group, Coastal Command, we listened out on the shipping wavelengths for reports of U-boat or surface raider attacks so that one of the Sunderlands, which were constantly on patrol, could be directed to assist. We didn't have a great deal of success.

It was during May that the war really came to me for the first time. Not required for duty until midnight I had gone to the camp cinema. I gradually became aware that the rhythm of the tap-dancing feet of Fred Astaire was being accompanied by an even louder rat-a-tat outside, seconds later came a loud hissing noise and the cinema doors burst open to reveal the fierce burning of incendiary bombs. The occupants of that cinema must have created a record for rapid evacuation. I was one of the first to a slit trench outside, a mistake as it happened because hot on my heels came the base commanding officer, a Group Captain, bellowing, "out of there, you lot! The bastards have dropped one on my car." They had. Parked across the road outside the Officer's Mess his car was beginning to blaze merrily. Some intrepid soul with a fire extinguisher fought the flames whilst the rest of us yelled encouragement and called, unsuccessfully, for someone to bring buckets of sand. A high pitched whistling sound heralded the fact that our adversaries aloft had decided to liven things up a little by changing from incendiaries to high explosive bombs. This time the Group Captain beat me to the slit trench. I only just made it. As I dived full length into the trench the blast of a nearby bomb lifted me out again. Lying for the next few minutes quivering and breathless I missed most of the tantrums of an apoplectic Group Captain. That bomb had scored a direct hit on his car. It had certainly put out the fire. In fact, all that could be found was part of the back seat and one wheel.

Any enthusiasm we had left for dealing with incendiary bombs was severely diminished when we realised that some of them were also fitted with explosive devices. Instead of spraying with water, or endeavouring to smother with sand, we simply slammed buckets of sand upside down over them and stood well back to await events. If the flames went out – good! If it exploded then, providing one dodged the flying bucket, all was well. This system worked perfectly until we ran out of buckets.

The Luftwaffe turned their full attention on Plymouth for four consecutive nights, by which time there was little left of the city centre. Naval dockyards and barracks suffered considerable damage, although at Mountbatten we escaped virtually unharmed. Despite my fear of the bombing I found that I hated the occasions when I was on duty in the bunker and, despite the earphones on my head, heard the dull crump of explosives outside and, worse still, felt the vibrations of the structure. From Mountbatten we had a clear view of the pier jutting out into the Sound blazing away spectacularly, even more so the main gasometer which had taken a direct hit and for a week had a flame like a huge Bunsen burner soaring up to a hundred feet above it. For some days our water supply at Mountbatten was cut off and the only drink available was the local cider. Whilst, at first, this was rather enjoyable I have never been able to face it since. After this, sporadic raids, both by night and day, continued throughout the war but never reached the ferocity of the 1941 blitz – I suppose there wasn't that much worth bombing left.

In June Nora travelled down by train to see me, staying in the base accommodation which had been made available for her. From Stockport station to Plymouth she was escorted by my very good friend, Jackie Bennett, who was returning from leave. During the war years trains could take up to fourteen hours on a journey such as this. Jackie came from Whaley Bridge and was the same age as myself, twenty-one and was also a wireless operator awaiting a vacancy on a gunnery course.

Always full of fun he pulled my leg unmercifully when he was given a date to join a gunnery school two weeks before the time I was to go myself. That meant he would get his sergeant's stripes that much sooner than me. Unfortunately, after passing the course and being posted to a Blenheim squadron, he was killed shortly afterwards on a daylight raid on, what was then a Luftwaffe airfield, Schipol (Amsterdam).

Nora was extremely fond of Jackie and very upset at the news of his death. I have never looked but you will probably find his name on the Whaley Bridge war memorial.

Late August 1941 and back I went to Yatesbury and the De Havilland Dominies for a brief refresher course on radio procedures. Then it was off to Number 5 Bombing and Gunnery school at Jurby on the Isle of Man. The timing of this was not very good insofar as my parents and Nora were concerned. The death of Jackie was quickly followed by that of a boy named Norman Raines, also a Wireless Operator/Air Gunner, whose home was in Chester Road, Poynton. Even worse he was flying from Jurby and in low cloud his aircraft crashed into Snaefell. Nora went to his funeral at Poynton church. What neither she, nor Norman's family ever knew, was that originally five bodies had been recovered from the wreckage and placed reverently in the coffins prior to despatch to their grieving relatives for burial. A re-check, however established that there had been six crew on board the aircraft, so another coffin was brought out of store and the bodies re-arranged.

After the sea trip from Liverpool to Douglas, Jurby situated in the north of the island, was eventually reached by, what in peacetime had been a tourist attraction, the rickety railway line from Douglas to Ramsey. It was never so busy as during those war years when it transported thousands of RAF personnel to and from the bombing and gunnery school.

The aircraft made available for training were Hampdens and Blenheims, all squadron time-expired and far from reliable. One flight in every three was said to end in disaster, usually engine failure resulting in minor accidents or fatality. This might have been an exaggeration, but from what I saw, not very much.

I was allocated to a Blenheim flight, not thankfully to the Hampdens. If the gunner's position in the Blenheim was cramped and uncomfortable the Hampden's was incomparably worse. The opening two flights I made from Jurby, apart from adding another eighty minutes to my flying experience were a waste of time. They were in an original version of the fighter bomber which had twin Vickers machine guns, fed by clipped-on ammunition pans each holding fifty rounds. One quick burst and the ammunition was exhausted. In the hydraulic Bristol gun turret employed the gunner had to lower the guns to be able to extract the pans from the breach of the gun and snap a new one into place. This meant that the muzzles of the guns would be elevated and a pursuing enemy fighter could throw caution to the winds and close in with impunity. After two flights in this type I then came a little more up to date by flights in the Mark IV Blenheim which, although fitted with belt-fed twin Browning machine guns, was still a long way from the four gun Fraser Nash turret which were now coming into use in the heavy bomber squadrons.

One snag in moving into this slightly more modern aircraft was that they were mainly flown by Polish pilots who threw the Blenheims all over the sky as if they were Spitfires. Whilst they complained of boredom I was scared out of my wits. Nevertheless, when flying with them there were never any problems with the aircraft, nor did I suffer the indignity of failure as on my first flight at Jurby when a "dropped cap" (a sliver of metal off the percussion cap being jammed in the firing pin, thus causing the gun to misfire) prevented me from carrying out the exercise. Like myself the aircraft and all its component parts did not want to spend any more time with those pilots than necessary. My shooting at the towed target drogues also improved. From an initial assessment of eight hits out of two hundred rounds fired I never scored less than ten with them, even reaching the dizzy heights of seventeen and nineteen. Although very pleased with myself on sober reflection I do not consider I was much of a threat to the Luftwaffe.

By October 1941 I had been in the Air Force just over a year and having amassed the grand total of 12 hours 50 minutes flying time, and given the non-substantive sergeant rank which, unless commissioned, was awarded to all aircrew. The trouble was, stop flying, for whatever reason, and the sergeant's stripes went too.

My pay now having been increased to eight shillings and sixpence (42½ pence) per day I went home on leave a comparatively rich man. Uniform resplendent with air gunner half wing, wireless operator lightning flashes badge and, of course three new stripes on each arm I was very proud of myself. I was totally unprepared for my reception when I arrived home on leave. On seeing me my mother and Nora both burst into tears. Losses in aircrew were, despite the censorship of the time becoming all too frequent and well known. It now seemed to them that I, too, was a prime candidate for those statistics. It didn't happen to everyone, I said, and it certainly wouldn't happen to me.

They remained unconvinced and I had a miserable ten days at home. At the end of it Nora said that unless I gave up flying any thought of marriage could be forgotten, she had no intention of being a young war widow. My mother agreed with her, refusing to accept that I could not simply tell the RAF that I no longer wished to have any active participation in the war.

I went to my next posting, at Kinloss, leaving behind a distraught mother and an ex-girl friend.

An Armstrong-Whitworth Whitley

CHAPTER 3

A Wedding Interlude

The final stage of aircrew training was an operational training unit. As a prospective member of a heavy bomber squadron I had been assigned to Kinloss where twin-engined Whitleys were based. The Whitley, popularly – and affectionately – known as "the flying coffin" because of their box-like fuselage and nose-down flying attitude had been one of the mainstays of Bomber Command having a greater range and bomb-carrying capacity than the Wellington which, generally had received much more publicity. The all-metal, sturdy construction of the Whitley was also more attractive to most aircrew (me included) than the geodetic fabric covered Wellington which, whilst also capable of absorbing punishment, was also that much more susceptible to fire.

Kinloss, near to the town of Forres, was the largest airfield complex I had yet seen. It had lengthy, wide tarmac runways, the main one into the prevailing wind giving a clear run over Findhorn Bay and out over the Moray Firth. I arrived there at the end of October 1941 and was immediately plunged into a series of lectures, Morse exercises and the basics of dead reckoning and astral navigation. Just in case, one of our cheerful instructors proclaimed, the real navigator was killed. What happened if the same fate became the pilot we asked. Not to worry he said, the aircraft would always come down!

Comments like this were not necessarily morale boosters. They didn't do my ears any good either, I developed an infection and was sent to the Royal Northern Infirmary,

Inverness, where I was admitted. I was there two weeks, during which time I flirted madly with any of the pretty young nurses who would give me the slightest encouragement. Very few did.

Whilst my ear problems improved there was concern about my general condition. So much so that the RAF Medical Officer came to the hospital and asked me if I really wished to carry on as aircrew. Like a fool, afraid of losing my non-substantive rank, I was adamant that I did. In an effort to get me back to peak fitness it was decided to send me to a Red Cross hospital, Darnaway Castle, for a period of convalescence. The home of Lord and Lady Moray it was a Scottish castle in the grand style. I had an enormous bedroom to myself, where every morning I was awakened by my own Red Cross nurse, Christina, with a cup of tea and, after bathing and shaving, escorted downstairs to a sumptuous breakfast. Lazy days followed, large lunches, afternoon teas and enormous dinners. I required little medical treatment, mainly drops in the ears. After a few days of this I was deemed fit enough to be included in the evening "going out" parties to either local dances or the cinema. Accompanied always by my nurse.

Twinges of conscience occasionally bothered me. Nearly all the patients, and there were Army and Navy as well as RAF, in Darnaway had serious disabilities, including the loss of sight or limbs, and I felt that I was not worthy of the care being so lavishly bestowed upon me.

I had also decided that I was madly in love with Christina.

So, time went by until my old friend, the Kinloss Medical Officer, came along to Darnaway so see how I was progressing. A quick examination confirmed his worst thoughts, "My God," he exclaimed, "what the hell you've been up to I don't know, but you're a damn sight worse than when I sent you here! Transport will be here at ten in the morning to take you back to the airfield. Be ready!"

Well, I was, and back at Kinloss just in time to apply for, and be granted Christmas leave. On the journey south I wasted a day in Glasgow looking desultorily in jewellers' windows at engagement rings and wondering if I took a train back up north and went to Darnaway if Christina would accept an offer of marriage. There seemed to be little point in going home, but it would not be fair to Mother if I did not go to see her and Dad. I could stop with them for a few days then come back to Scotland. That, I decided, was a good idea.

After an emotional welcome Mother stood back and had a long hard look at me. "So, you've been ill, and now you're supposed to be fit. You don't look it. What have you been up to?"

I don't know what it is about most mothers, but they only have to look at you and ask a simple question and you find yourself pouring your heart out. I told her about my Red Cross nurse and that I was going to ask Christina to marry me.

"And you are still flying?"

I nodded.

"Then nothing has changed has it? You would be better marrying Nora as you first intended."

"But, she won't have me."

"She will, and she'll be here within the hour to tell you so." So she was.

Our reconciliation was rewarded by huge smiles from my watching Dad and approving Mother, who then announced that the wedding had been arranged for January 21st 1942, the anniversary of Nora's mother's birthday. As soon as I returned to Kinloss I must inform the RAF that more leave would be required to enable me to attend this important ceremony.

I was slow to realise it at the time, but Mother's seemingly uncanny intuition over my carryings-on in Scotland was no such thing. That RAF Medical Officer had a lot to answer for.

So, everything was fixed, although for a brief interval – thanks to the war – I thought I had a reprieve. For quite a while there had been three major Nazi warships, the Scharnhorst, the Gneisnau and the Prinz Eugen, bottled up in the port of Brest. Intelligence reports suggested a breakout back to German ports by these vessels could be anticipated late January or early February. Their obvious course would take them between Iceland and the north of Scotland, in which case aircraft based at Kinloss would have a vital role to play. I was called into the Flight office one morning and instructed to start my leave that day, January 10th and report back on the 17th. The telegram I sent home told of my joy at being with all my loved ones within the next twenty-four hours and my deep sorrow that the wedding would have to be postponed. I had badly underestimated the resilience of both my mother and Nora. When I arrived home it was to discover that the marriage ceremony had been re-arranged for the fourteenth.

On the day I had a beautiful bride. Looking at the only photograph allowed under wartime restrictions you would not realise that under her wedding gown the bride is wearing a cricketer's white sweater. It was a bitter winter's day, snowing and the church had no heat. There was a moment of panic as my best man, Jack Rothwell, dropped the wedding ring at the crucial moment. Quite understandable really, he was wearing woollen gloves.

The reception was at the Brookfield cafe in the village. I suspect the food served broke all the regulations in force at the time, Nora's farmer father, Jim, made sure that the guests were well fed. During the war the cafe was very popular, especially when the US Air Force came to nearby Hope Green and the dances there organised by an elderly village gentleman named Dick Clayton who, during the war, did a great job keeping up the morale of the youngsters.

The honeymoon, in Blackpool, was another example of my extraordinary good luck during the war. It snowed, and it snowed, and it snowed..... When we went out for a walk our footprints in the snow were the only ones along the length of the promenade. Conditions were so bad that the rail services were cancelled and there was no way I could return either to Poynton or Kinloss. As a result I got a ten days extension of leave and, when I did eventually arrive back in Scotland, the Scharnhorst, Gneisnau and Prinz Eugen obligingly, for the Kinloss boys, took everyone by surprise and came through the

A Wedding Interlude

English Channel. During the action which ensued amongst other attacks on the German vessels was one by a squadron of twelve Swordfish torpedo bombers from a South coast base. It was ineffective, all the Swordfish were shot down and I do not think there were any survivors.

CHAPTER 4

"Ops" Flight

Returning to Kinloss at the end of January 1942 for the next four weeks I was what was popularly known as a "spare body." Being so long away from the airfield my name had been deleted from the training programme to which I had originally been assigned. I had to wait until another suitable slot could be found. Meanwhile I was kept occupied twenty-four out of every forty-eight hours as Orderly Sergeant. Briefly summed up, this meant attending parades, including those for the sick, the lame and the lazy, making sure the guard room and its occupants were awake when they should be and being at the beck and call of the Orderly Officer. As he was usually a disgruntled grounded pilot that meant finding a quiet, secluded bed where he could spend his duty time in restful peace.

What at first seemed to be a "perk" of the job turned out to be anything but. As Orderly Sergeant I was not supposed to fraternise with my fellow sergeants who lived and slept in Nissen huts with a red-hot stove belting out heat during the cold winter nights. Instead I was allocated a small room in a wooden hut where, with no fire, I would lie fully dressed in my bed, and, despite the addition of a greatcoat on top of the woollen blankets would spend the night shivering. My next door neighbour, also a WOP/AG sergeant, like myself temporarily out of the training stream and awaiting the opportunity to move on, suffered likewise. However, being a member of the Salvation Army he was more philosophical saying that it was part of life's pattern and things could only get better.

Kinloss was, perhaps, the largest airfield in northern Britain and, in addition to its function as an operational training unit was occasionally used for sorties on targets in Norway. One afternoon four-engined Halifax heavy bombers of 35 squadron arrived from their base down south to be re-fuelled and loaded with a new type of mine destined to damage or, hopefully destroy, the German battleship Tirpitz which was sheltering in a Norwegian fiord. These mines protruded out from the bomb-bays of the Halifax seemingly only inches clear of the ground. As the aircraft roared down the runway on takeoff, for what resulted in a disastrous raid, the whole of Kinloss breathed a sigh of relief when the heavy-laden bombers struggled free of the ground without incident.

I never thought that one of the duties of Orderly Sergeant would be that of dog-minder but just before going out to his aircraft one of the squadron's rear gunners came to me carrying in his arms a Yorkshire terrier. "This is Flak," he said, "our mascot who likes to fly with us. But he's not going any further on this trip. Please look after him until we get back." I looked after the little fellow for over a week until arrangements were made to send him to the rear gunner's family. Together with the rest of his crew he didn't come back.

The end of February and my name was listed for a course beginning on March 1st. For the first time I flew in a Whitley, one of the older Mark IV type which had operated over Germany and survived to tell the tale. Fully equipped with the latest radio equipment, front and tail gun turrets armed with two and four Browning ·303 belt-fed machine guns, each capable of firing 1100 rounds per minute it was very impressive to a newly-fledged Wireless Operator/Air Gunner, especially the armament. That was until we heard how inferior the bomber's defences were when attacked by an enemy fighter's 20mm cannon shells which, in addition to the heavier calibre had twice the effective range. This was a serious fault on British bombers, remaining uncorrected throughout the war and the cause of many of the heavy losses.

About this time I was granted a 48 hour pass. Not long enough to go home, so I agreed with three other sergeants that we would have a pleasant cultural break in Glasgow. Having sent brief letters to Nora and my mother, expressing regret that two days made it impossible to travel any further south and that I had booked into one of the large city centre hotels. It was a great pity that they would be unable to join me there. So, having done my duty, as I saw it, off I went with a clear conscience determined to enjoy myself. On the first night, together with my companions, this I certainly did. The following morning, about 11am, we were sitting in the hotel dining room striving to clear plates of the huge breakfasts of bacon, egg, black pudding and toast which the kindly staff had concocted for us. We had refused both tea and coffee, deciding that pints of beer would be of more assistance to our digestive tracts. I had my glass to my lips when suddenly I became aware that Mother was amongst those present.

A small measure of port wine at Christmas being her one and only venture into alcoholism it was a terrible shock to discover her beloved offspring partaking of the demon drink at that time of the day. She obviously paled, so much so that the manager who had escorted her into the room asked her if she would like a brandy. That really did not make the situation any better!

The situation was eased when Nora, having freshened up after the long night train journey, also came into the room. Within minutes they were both sat at the table with us drinking tea and chatting with the other boys as if they were old friends, before they left and went off for some more cultural education.

Two memories remain with me of the short time we had together as the next morning Nora and Mother left to the south and home, I north to Kinloss. One was a show at the Argylle theatre, where the great Will Fyffe tugged at the audience's emotional heartstrings, and the other was Mother's foray into a chemist's shop. Here she asked for a packet of Rendells. The assistant looked at her and asked them is she wanted them for herself. In a very dignified, but somewhat haughty manner, Mother stated that the overnight train journey had given her severe indigestion and she needed the Rendells for relief.

"Madame," said the girl behind the counter, "what you did on the train is none of my business, but Rendells are a contraceptive pessary. Are you sure you don't mean Rennies?"

During the month of March my log book shows that I did ten training flights, nearly all in daylight, in either this, or the later version Mark V type of Whitley. Ahead of me, just behind the pilot in the cockpit a trainee navigator sat at his table busily plotting our course and feverishly checking the little information I could feed to him through my own endeavours. At this stage of the proceedings this mainly consisted of my reporting "QDM's" from base. Translated from the "Q" code this read: "Your magnetic course to steer with zero wind to reach me is........." Not all that much use to him really as we could be flying in any direction except towards base – and we were not sure what the wind strength and direction was anyway. Still, it did allow him to draw another line on his chart from the airfield into outer space, where with a bit of luck, somewhere along that line we *might* be. The navigator was obviously comforted and grateful for this fairly useless information; I was happy too. My own work, recorded by base looked well in my log book. The pilots on these flights were always experienced peacetime regulars who had been brought out of retirement to assist in training programmes. Totally unflappable they ignored most of the information supplied by their hard-working crew and flew sublimely round the prescribed course by a mixture of map-reading and intuition.

By the time March was over I had recorded over 30 hours of daylight flying and almost four hours of night-time. Little wonder that Hitler was reported to be concerned about the growing might of the RAF! The first few days of April were hectic. Lectures and ground simulation exercises were interspersed with flights in an Anson wherein, aided by a yet another trainee navigator, I almost succeeded in making the elderly (must have been in their thirties) pilots unsure of their

Author Kinloss

position. What I remember mostly about this stage is the feeling of total exposure in the perspex covered crew space, the stomach-churning bumps and sideslips the rough weather at the time produced and, possibly induced by the all-round view of nothing from the Anson's glasshouse cockpit during the hours of darkness over blacked-out Britain, the feeling of utter desolation as if the world outside no longer existed.

However, possibly aided by an accurate "fix" when we were struggling to find our way one tempestuous night on April 6th I was told that I had successfully completed the course and would now be transferred to an operational flight. This, of course was still at 19 OTU Kinloss and not a bomber squadron, although in certain circumstances we could be called on to participate in actual bombing raids. This never happened to me, although a little while later crews from some "Ops Flights" at OTU were involved in the thousand bomber raid on Cologne.

My flying hours had now grown to almost forty-four hours day and eighteen by night. Back on the Whitleys after three testing flights with an experienced pilot I was told to report to the main hangar at ten the following day and not to leave until I had become a member of a would-be bomber crew.

The making-up of crews was a hit-and-miss affair when a batch of trainee pilots, navigators, wireless operators and air gunners were assembled in one of the hangars and left to sort themselves out. Naturally gravitating into their own particular trade groups each one regarded the others suspiciously. Then the pilots took the initiative, one by one, in selecting a navigator. As a wireless operator, and not in the priority category, I stood on the fringe of my own group trying to look intelligent and hoping that some kind soul, preferably two gifted aviators, would be suitably impressed and adopt me. My prayers were answered. A pilot and a navigator, both officers, approached me. "This one looks almost human," said the pilot, "what's your rating in Morse son?" When I answered twenty-two words a minute, which was fairly fast, they looked suitably impressed. "And," asked the navigator, "what about your gunnery?" The truth had to be told. "Only average," I admitted. The pilot grinned. "That'll do me," he said, "I've no intention of ever allowing a German to get within shooting distance of any aircraft I'm flying. Welcome to my crew. My name is Dawes and this navigator I've just recruited is called Keeler. You're a lucky lad."

I thought that he was right, only the very best were given commissions on training courses and I had been fortunate enough to be selected by two of them.

The final addition to our team, a rear gunner, was a reticent Yorkshire lad who none of us got to know well, we flew together for the rest of April until the end of the first week in May. Apart from the gunner who, I suspected was asleep in his turret most of the time, I was quite content. Only once were we in real trouble, that was when we were lost somewhere to the north of Cape Wrath, in very bad weather, on the night of April 30th. Fortunately the radio gear worked perfectly and with aid of positional "fixes" and bearings from ground stations we made our way safely back to Kinloss. I was quite proud when during this time I was able to answer the query of a caring Waaf in flying control, "Are you OK?" I could answer "Yes," and as an added compliment transmitted the code signal meaning "Your Morse is good." You never know with the girls when a little flattery will pay dividends.

The course terminated with bombing exercises on an infrared target located, I think, in the vicinity of Inverurie. That's where we went anyway and because our aim must not have been more than the two miles astray, as was normal in those days, we were classified as ready for squadron service.

The part of the bombing exercise which worried me most was the launching of the photo-flash bombs. These were the responsibility of the wireless operator and meant crawling under the main petrol tank from my cosy radio position, down the vibrating pitch-black fuselage to the flare-chute. Above here were strapped the photo-flashes. All one had to do, in the blackness was to undo the straps, lift the flare, which was over three feet long and weighed some five kilos, and place it in the mouth of the flare-chute – being careful not to let it go. Before that happened a piece of string had to be fastened, one end to the safety pin in the tail of the flare and the other to any convenient point in the aircraft. Convenient! And all in total darkness, with hands freezing in the cold even though we wore silk gloves to prevent frostbite ! However, having tied the string and hanging on like grim death to save the flare sliding prematurely down the chute, on hearing the magic words over the intercom "Bombs away" the flare was released. Depending on the height at which this happened and the calculated time-lapse before the bombs hit the ground, the theory was for the flare to explode at the same moment. So, according to the height flown, the necessary delay for launching was calculated in seconds before pushing the flare down the chute. If all went well the flare would leave the aircraft, the string would pull out the safety pin and a thousand feet or so later the flare would ignite, illuminating the target bombed, the camera would click and you had proof of your success or otherwise. Ah, the wonders of the technology of those days! Sadly it did not always work that way. Sometimes the string, after pulling out the safety pin, in some mysterious way, was loth to part company with the flare which then ignited and had a nasty habit of looping over the tailplane revealing the bomber to delighted German flak gunners on the ground, and creating extreme consternation to the aircraft's rear gunner. Worse still, the flare could shoot back up the chute and its fierce incandescent glare would horribly burn and possibly permanently blind the wireless operator.

There was little leisure time during this stage of training. There was no way I could get to Darnaway Castle, but I did call in at the Royal Northern Infirmary, Inverness, in an attempt to obtain information about Christina. All to no avail and I never heard from, or saw her, again. A visit to the town's cinema and I met Vicki (short for Victoria) and a week later had another enjoyable day with her. A petite brunette, she was a nice girl too. However, I was to leave Kinloss very soon – which, perhaps, was just as well.

CHAPTER 5

51 Squadron

The first week in May 1942 brought a flurry of activity as the course ended with four flights in as many days, myself to blaze away a reasonable amount of ammunition to prove that my gunnery remained constantly average and the navigator to demonstrate that with his guidance we could drop bombs two miles from the target like everyone else.

At this time we had been given sleeping quarters in comfortable wooden huts some four miles away from the airfield in woods at Balnageith, a village just outside Forres. Our training finally completed, we spent several lazy days here in the fine and warm weather whilst we awaited our fate in the form of a posting to an operational squadron. When it eventually came it was to 51 squadron of Bomber Command, not only us, but all the other crews who were at the same state of readiness as ourselves. We assured ourselves that this somewhat unusual event was because the squadron was building up strength and not to replace heavy casualties. We did not consider that it was only the latter which would necessitate the former.

It did not take us long to discover that 51 squadron, comprised of twin-engined Whitleys had quite a reputation. At the outbreak of war the squadron had been based at Driffield in East Yorkshire. In the summer of 1940 this airfield was subjected to heavy attacks by the Luftwaffe resulting in losses to both aircraft and ground personnel as a consequence of which a move further inland to Dishforth (twenty miles from Wetherby, where I went to live in 1976) was deemed prudent. From this location, over the following eighteen months 51 squadron carried out operations against Germany and Italy. Flying time on the latter was in the region of thirteen hours. Heavily laden, mainly with petrol, the lumbersome bombers took much longer to become airborne, and the main trunk road running alongside the airfield, the A1 (or Great North Road as it was then known) had to be closed as the aircraft lifted off the very end of the runway and roared across it at no more than a few feet high. The thrills for the crews did not finish there for, on reaching the dizzy height of maybe 10,000 feet by the time they had crossed France the Whitleys were confronted by the Alps. Unable to go over them the bombers had to gingerly negotiate a safe path through them. A hair-raising task, even if the moon happened to break through the clouds at the right moment. The Whitley was the only bomber capable of reaching Italy at this stage of the war and the one consolation their crews had for this dubious honour was that the Italians were possibly more terrified of them coming than they were of going.

The first combined operations raid was also amongst the squadron's honours when paratroopers were dropped on the Bruneval radar station in northern France and, less successfully, provided a diversionary bombing sortie for the commando raid on St Nazaire.

All this was before my time. As I joined them 51 squadron were in the process of vacating their Dishforth home and moving to Chivenor, in North Devon.

Four miles from the town of Barnstaple Chivenor airfield was bounded to the north by the road from that town to Ilfracombe, and to the south by the River Taw. From the wooden hut which was my "B" flight dispersal headquarters at the side of the main runway, there was a clear view across the river to Appledore and Bideford.

At this stage of the war Chivenor's chief claim to fame was the capture of an almost brand new, undamaged Luftwaffe bomber complete with crew. Liverpool had been their target for the night, where they claimed to have dropped their bombs. There must be an element of doubt about this as they became completely disorientated on their return journey to base in northern France and mistook the Bristol for the English Channel. Thankfully seeing a lit flare path on crossing the coast they made a perfect landing and taxied up to the control tower, switched off the engines and climbed out of the aircraft to find themselves surrounded by RAF personnel. There was quite a fight, not between the British and the Germans, but the furious Luftwaffe pilot and his navigator.

51 Squadron: crew room Chivenor 1942

During the five months I was to spend at Chivenor the weather was mainly dry, sunny and warm. When stood down from operations I would either walk into Barnstaple to the cinema there or go the opposite direction to Braunton where the local ladies had established a marvellous canteen in the village hall. Scrumptious home-made buttered scones were in plentiful supply and occasionally, supplied by anonymous farmer friends, even bacon and eggs were on the menu. I got into the habit of going here quite often with two of my closest friends, Sid Hodges from Wellingborough and a fair-haired Scot from Edinburgh, Bill Dudgeon.

One of the middle-aged ladies at the canteen seemed to take pity on the three young airmen who were always grateful for the friendly atmosphere and would eat all the buttered scones offered. She invited us to visit her home, any evening we desired, to meet her husband and family. Home was a farm up in the hills overlooking the airfield. The husband made us very welcome and, very formally, proudly introduced us to the family – two boys, aged eight and ten years and two girls thirteen and seventeen.

They were all devout members of the religious sect Plymouth Brethren. They neither drank nor smoked and none of them had ever been to a cinema or listened to the radio. Their beliefs meant that they were conscientious objectors but they were always wonderful to we three, whose aim in life was to drop bombs on other humans, and whenever our nerves demanded some kind of relief there was no better way than to visit them.

Always they gave us supper, after which we would assemble round the piano and as the elder daughter, Ruth, played would join lustily in singing the hymns. My favourite was "The Old Rugged Cross". Whenever I hear it today it brings back the memory of those evenings so long ago. My regret is that when I left Chivenor I never had the chance to say goodbye and to say how grateful I was for their friendship.

The war had not been going well at all, perhaps the main area of concern was the Battle of the Atlantic where the Germans were gaining the upper hand. With bases at the west French Biscay ports of Brest, La Rochelle, La Pallice, Lorient St Nazaire, Bordeaux and elsewhere enemy submarines were creating havoc with Allied shipping and the outlook was ominous unless something was quickly done.

One of the measures was to introduce daylight aircraft sweeps down the Bay of Biscay. At best a U-boat might be sighted, attacked and sunk. At the very least, if intercepted, they would be forced to dive and not be able to carry on across the Bay at full speed. This would have the effect of shortening their range and endurance in the Atlantic thus using up more fuel and lessening the time they had in which to hunt our shipping.

For this purpose the Whitleys of 51 squadron, now becoming obsolete for operations over Germany, were detached (or "lent") to Coastal Command pending the squadron's conversion to the four-engined Halifax bomber. This was the situation when, with the rest of the re-inforcing crews I arrived at Chivenor from Kinloss.

To our dismay we were immediately split up as crews and re-allocated to the more experienced veterans of the squadron. The first flight I had with one of them, a Sergeant Harris, hardly inspired me with confidence. On takeoff he managed to scrape the runway with the port engine airscrew, a difficult feat to accomplish, and an extremely erratic circuit of the airfield followed which ended with a very heavy landing. According to my log book we were airborne for only ten minutes. It seemed much longer at the time. I never saw, let alone flew with that particular pilot again. I think, possibly, he was given early retirement.

My remaining flights that month were with two men who were to be pilot and copilot of the crew with whom I was to operate in the Bay of Biscay. The skipper, Sergeant Bartlett, was a soft-spoken Devonian from Budleigh Salterton. All aircrew had their superstitions, his was to sing "We're off to see the Wizard" (from the film "The Wizard of Oz") as we went charging down the runway on takeoff. Months later, after I had left his crew, he must have forgotten to sing it on one occasion. His name is on the Budleigh Salterton War Memorial.

The other pilot, Flight Sergeant Acree, was an American who had enlisted in the Royal Canadian Air Force prior to the entry of the United States into the war. Originally he had been flying Wellington bombers but his transfer to 51 squadron and his lack of experience in flying Whitleys meant that, although superior in rank, he flew as second pilot. This never bothered him, he was an easy-going friendly soul and, due to his advanced years (thirty-one) was known to all and sundry as "Pop." I suspect he rather liked it.

Our navigator was a curly-haired blond lad from South Wales. His surname was Battle, so he answered to "Fairy," after the aircraft of that name. Good at his job he was too, we forgave him for the incident when after one long trip he announced that we were homing on Bishop Rock lighthouse only to discover from the up-coming fireworks that we were on the approaches to Brest.

Reg Smart was the rear gunner. A Londoner he was always alert and accurate with the four Browning machine guns in the Fraser Nash turret. Between them they pumped out 4,400 rounds a minute, but they were no match either in range or effectiveness against enemy fighters with 20mm cannon.

The final member of our crew was another Wireless/Operator Air Gunner, whose name I will not mention for reasons which will become obvious later.

So there we were, a crew with ages ranging from the early thirties to eighteen. Although we knew, in 1942, that the Whitley was becoming obsolete as more and more of the four-engined Stirlings, Halifaxes and Lancasters came into service we still had every confidence in our own aircraft. This despite the pundits who proclaimed that using them for daylight patrols over the Bay of Biscay was just a simple and effective method of disposing of them. Unfortunately, events were to show that they may have had a point.

My log book shows that on May 30th we were sent on a submarine identification flight off the South Devon coast. This turned out to be the British submarine "Thunderbolt," which had originally been named "Thetis" and sank whilst on acceptance trials off Llandudno with heavy loss of life in, I think, 1937. Salvaged and re-named "Thunderbolt" she never had much luck and, when based on Malta, was sunk by the Italians in 1943 with the loss of all on board her.

The last day of May 1942 proved the worth of both our pilots. Briefed for our first operational sortie and fully loaded with petrol and bombs we had serious engine trouble after takeoff, but their cool efficient handling ensured a safe landing and, after that, the crew placed a 100% trust in the Bartlett/Acree combination.

June, and seven daylight sorties down the Bay. It may be difficult to envisage what flying was like in those days. No pressurised cabins, just draughty, often bitterly cold and always noisy aircraft. The Biscay sweeps meant never exceeding altitudes of 1,000 feet so as to avoid being tracked by enemy radar. This mainly mitigated the cold but left little chance of recovery if there were engine trouble. The cruising speed of the Whitley at this height was about 160 miles an hour with no head wind, and as the patrols went down as far as the north coast of Spain extra fuel tanks had to be fitted.

The start of each patrol I found a pleasure and usually manned the front turret so that I had the best view possible of this beautiful part of Britain. Gaining height after takeoff we passed first between Hartland Point and Lundy island, then down the Cornish coast and out over the Isles of Scilly. The varying colours of the water from deep blue to emerald green always intrigued me. This state of euphoria was not allowed to last long. The Luftwaffe too was apt to come looking at the scenery hereabouts.

As we left the Isles of Scilly behind us and approached Bishop Rock lighthouse the sky around us was scanned ever more anxiously. It was on this precise point that the patrols were formulated. Bishop Rock was designated as the base of a fan, the blade tips of which stretched out to the northern Spanish coast touching La Corunna, Gijon, Santander, Bilbao and San Sebastian. Each fan blade was a beat of the Bay of Biscay patrols, and at briefing everyone prayed that they would be allocated one of the more Westerly ones. The one least liked was Bishop Rock – Bilbao – San Sebastian – Bishop Rock. The most southerly leg of this duty came perilously close to the Luftwaffe bases around Bordeaux, and in addition to silent pleas to God, mascots were implored by worried crews to ensure that one of the safer beats towards Corunna would be given to them.

Patrols lasted anything between eight and nine hours. We normally flew to just within visual distance of the Spanish coast, keeping an eye open for any possible blockade runners coming in from the Atlantic and creeping along inshore to the haven of a friendly port in western France. There were none of today's more sophisticated navigational aids. The wireless operator gave some assistance by giving bearings on various radio stations or beacons, and in dire emergencies courses to steer to reach airfields in England, always providing that they were within radio range. At night, if conditions were favourable positions could be plotted by using the sextant for star-sights but, of course, on daylight flights this was not an option open to the navigator.

The strain of low flying, plus the constant watch for U-boats and German aircraft which were also patrolling looking for us, meant that we were very weary aircrews when we returned to base. Some of us never did, they simply flew down the Bay south from Bishop Rock and we never knew what happened to them. It could have been engine failure, or fighter interception by the Luftwaffe. One exception was a Whitley in which my old Salvation Army friend from Kinloss was the Wireless Operator. On patrol ourselves we picked up a radio message saying they had trouble and would have to "ditch" (force-landing on the sea). We were flying on an adjacent leg and a quick calculation showed we could reach them in only ten minutes flying time. We did, just as the stricken aircraft alighted on a dead calm sea with a huge splash. The crew must have been alright as the top escape hatch opened and someone began to climb out. Then there was an almighty explosion and when the spray and smoke cleared there was nothing – no debris – nothing. They had forgotten to jettison their Torpex depth charges before ditching and water pressure had triggered off the bombs.

After we had landed back at base two of us had the difficult task of telling the wife of a member of the lost crew that her husband had been killed. She didn't believe us and months later when the squadron left Chivenor the lady still lived in her rented room in nearby Braunton confidently waiting her husband's return.

Another sad event at this time, due to a forced landing in the Bristol Channel was the death of a popular Canadian Wireless Operator, named MacDonald, from Toronto. On impact he unfortunately suffered a broken leg. All the crew got safely out of the bomber into the dinghy before the aircraft sank. The weather was, however, atrocious, gale force wind and driving rain and, although the crash position was known the dinghy could not be found that day.

The following morning the weather eased and the Clovelly lifeboat located them, they were all alright – except MacDonald. The father of a boy who had been born to his wife after he left Canada, he had died during the night from exposure. The little church on a hill overlooking the airfield in the village of Heanton Puchardon has his grave.

On June 22nd I filled in a temporary vacancy with another crew and were way down the Bay when we spotted a U-boat on the surface. Visibility was very good at the time and the German lookouts must have been wide-awake for the submarine crash-dived before we could get anywhere near him.

Along came July 1st and as we were due for leave to start the following day we went to briefing that morning praying that we would be allocated to one of the more westerly legs of the patrol. Naturally – we weren't. It was the dreaded close-in to the French coast beat. That day we were ultra-cautious but, in our favourite aircraft "S" for Sugar the trip went without incident.

The next morning found us at Barnstaple railway station on our various ways to wherever we were going to spend the next fourteen days. I, of course, was off home to my wife. Apart from a brief weekend we had spent together in Glasgow, whilst I was based in Kinloss I had not seen Nora since our honeymoon.

After the usual rapturous welcome from my mother, I settled down with Nora and we had a wonderful two weeks during which we visited Blackpool again and our old honeymoon hotel. After what we thought was a serious discussion we decided to start a family. Looking back at the circumstances of the time it was a foolish decision – but there we are and nine months later along came my son Bryan.

Back from leave, and July passed uneventfully with only two further Biscay patrols towards the end of that month. August began with a couple of operations in three days, the second one on August 3rd bringing us some short-lived fame and tattered nerves.

Unhappy at having been allocated one of the more inshore legs of the Biscay sweep we were relieved to have reached the most southerly point of the operation and be heading north up the Bay. On duty at the radio set I was suddenly alerted by "Pop" Acree gesticulating frantically through the starboard side window of the cockpit. There on the surface, about five miles away, was a U-boat. Pounding away at a high speed, with a white wash streaming out astern, he had not yet seen us. At the controls Bartlett turned into the attack. Simultaneously my fellow WOP/AG who was in the front gun turret decided he would prefer to be located elsewhere. Behind the radio equipment seemed to be his overwhelming desire and the changeover must have created some sort of RAF record. Suffice it to say that within seconds he was the wireless operator and I was the front gunner.

As we neared the target he saw us and began to dive. I opened up with the two Brownings in the front turret but, apart from irritating the poor devils as they scrambled down the conning tower hatch, I doubt if I caused much harm.

Possibly the six Torpex depth charges we dropped did. These were designed to destroy, or damage, any target within a range and depth of fifty feet. We still had one weapon left, an armour piercing bomb which the theorists told us we could drop from a height of a thousand feet and sink any surfaced U-boat. With our bombing record we hadn't got a lot of faith in this, but it was never put to the test. The submarine did not re-surface and whether we sank, or even damaged it, we never knew. We circled the area for some twenty minutes, which was as long as we dared if we hoped to get back to base with our remaining fuel.

U-boat Attack, August 1942

Landing back at Chivenor we found quite a crowd waiting for us. After weeks of seemingly ineffectual patrolling by the squadron there had at last been some positive action.

This incident kept us out of operations for over three weeks. The powers-that-be thought much more about the occurrence than we did. De-briefing followed de-briefing culminating in personal congratulations from the Commanding Officer at Coastal Command Headquarters,

Northwood, London. A rare honour indeed for a Bomber Command crew! Bartlett was promoted to Flight Sergeant and "Pop" Acree to Warrant Officer. As a crew we took advantage of the visit to Northwood to spend two nights in London to celebrate their promotion, and our survival.

Better still, on reporting back to the squadron at Chivenor we were granted seven days special leave. Despite the risks involved, hunting for U-boats had its rewards!

My wife, Nora, and my parents, delighted to see me as they were, suspected that there must be a reason for my appearance so soon after my previous visit. I don't know why, but I never told them about the U-boat and I discovered afterwards that, with the exception of my fellow WOP/AG, neither did the rest of the crew tell anyone at home. I suppose it was our idea to avoid giving them cause to worry about us, but I'm not sure we succeeded. Certainly that old soldier, my Dad, had his suspicions. Years later, when we did talk about it, he said. "Son, the stress showed in your face. To me, when you came home on that leave you had aged ten years."

CHAPTER 6

Trouble Begins

When we did return to the squadron it was to find that there had, inevitably been changes. There were new faces in the Mess, replacements for losses over the previous three weeks. Four "B" flight crews to whom we had felt particular close had flown off down the Bay and simply disappeared. Fighters? Engine trouble? A sudden encounter with a U-boat or surface raider? We never knew.

The only bit of good news was that both Bill Dudgeon and Sid Hodges were still with us and had, so far escaped unscathed.

My first flight on returning was with one of the replacement pilots, a Sergeant Whitworth. It was an exercise in one-engine flying which, in a Whitley, was aerodynamically like dragging a motorised dustbin round the sky with a lead weight attached. The boy, he would not be twenty years old, did very well, managing to stay airborne and fly the prescribed course before, after an hour, landing without breaking anything. He beamed with satisfaction when I complimented him, no doubt thinking it wonderful he had gained the approval of someone like myself, who had not only over two hundred hours flying time but had survived three months with an operational squadron.

The following day, August 27th 1942, came our first patrol after the U-boat episode. Takeoff time was unusually late at 1506 and would have meant a night landing on return. For this trip we could not have "S" for Sugar, our favourite

Whitley, instead we were allocated "Y" York which we had used before but had not been favourably impressed. Our misgivings were justified when, after being airborne for an hour and leaving Bishop Rock the starboard engine began to make the most alarming noises and misfire. A hurried debate between our two pilots and "Fairy" Battle the navigator ended with the decision to jettison our bombload before gingerly turning on the good port engine and returning to Chivenor where we landed safely nearly two hours later. Frustrating, because much of the stress occurred not by the actual operation itself but by the tension of pre-flight briefings and takeoffs with bombers heavily laden with petrol and high explosives. An aborted mission such as this one in "Y" York counted for nothing in the struggle to have thirty operations in our log books, after which we would be "stood down" to act as instructors for a period of six months. Theoretically that *might* mean six months longer to live.

We flew "Y" York twice more over the next three days on flights to the nearby St Eval airfield and although the fitters had worked hard on her neither Bartlett nor Acree were very happy. It was with great relief that for our last patrol of the month, on August 31st, we got back our beloved "S" for Sugar. The trip was uneventful, but unknown to me things were to soon go sadly wrong.

On September 2nd, about halfway down the Bay, on what we thought to be one of the safer legs of the patrols, we were intercepted by four JU 88's. Possibly the most versatile aircraft of the war we were lucky to get away from them. Only some superb sea level flying by our skipper, making accurate attacks by the 88's difficult, saved our skins. Reg Smart, our rear gunner, claimed to have damaged two of our assailants. My fellow Wireless Operator had, of course, got himself behind the radio gear again (I could never imagine what sort of protection that was – it was next to the main petrol tank). In the front turret I was cross-eyed trying to get in effective bursts with my two guns as I had fleet-second glimpses of 88's as they peeled off after, with their superior speed, they zoomed from behind to pass ahead of us. I couldn't claim any hits, but I certainly used up a lot of ammunition. The duration of the attacks was short-lived and the enemy turned away towards France. We assumed that they must have been at the limit of their endurance and were very low on fuel.

None of our crew were hurt but our aircraft, poor old "S for Sugar" suffered some damage and was never the same again. We took her up on another patrol two days later, but she wasn't having any of it and we were back at base an hour later with engine trouble.

My log book shows that the powers-that-be thought some intensified training would not come amiss at this stage. On the other side of the Bristol Channel from Chivenor, in the Tenby region of South Wales, was an airfield called Carew Cheriton. Here Warrant Officer "Pop" Acree and I were the leading lights in a series of flights involving low level bombing and cine-gun exercises with Spitfires. Our line-shooting and popularity with the local WAAFS (the ladies of the RAF) came to an abrupt finale when one day, on landing, we hit a lorry which had strayed on to the runway. That not only decapitated the driver but didn't do our Whitley a great deal of good either. It was a somewhat subdued Acree and Goodwin who returned to Chivenor the following day.

Waiting here anxiously for us was Bartlett who wanted us back in his crew for an early patrol the next morning. The flight was long and tedious, but entirely without incident. I did not know it then but this was to be the last time we were to fly together The aircraft letter was "E," an omen maybe.

The following afternoon I was detailed to fly on an air test with a newly-arrived Pilot Officer. The Barnstaple branch of the Air Training Corps, always eager to gain flying experience, had contrived to get authority to get their members aboard any local flights. Consequently, on this occasion, I found myself being trailed across the airfield to the aircraft by six hero-worshipping youngsters of fourteen to sixteen years of age. Rather than trailing, waddled would be a better word to describe their progress. As ordained in regulations each boy was uncomfortably equipped with parachute harness, Mae West and a flying helmet. I checked them as they laboriously clambered aboard but failed to notice that one of them had been dragging the plug on the end of his helmet communication lead through the wet grass on his way across the airfield.

I was far from enthusiastic at their presence. Although the chances were remote, there was always a possibility that an unwelcome member of the Luftwaffe would creep in and join the party – with possibly disastrous results.

My presentiment of disaster appeared to be coming true when, after the pilot fully opening the throttles, we charged off down the runway. We were approaching flying speed when, back in the fuselage, one of the Air Cadets discovered an inter-communication socket by the flare-chute and promptly plugged in. Murphy's Law ensured that this was the damp one which had been dragged through the wet grass.

The short-circuit created a loud howl in our headphones which was just the same as an undercarriage failure warning. The pilot cut the engines and slammed hard on the brakes. We came to shuddering halt with smoking tyres yards from the perimeter fence with the sirens of the fire tender and ambulance rapidly approaching, and the language of our irate skipper becoming more and more colourful as he regained his breath.

After that I was even less enthusiastic about the Air Training Corps.

The next day my dignity was somewhat restored when I had the compliment of being detailed to fly with the Commanding Officer, Squadron Leader Tony Meade. Because of his administrative responsibilities his number of operational sorties were restricted and he rarely contrived to more than one every four or five weeks. Whenever he did he selected a crew and went out looking for trouble, all too often he found it. The day I flew with him he was, thankfully, unlucky and we came back never having fired a shot, better still nobody had fired at us either. Sadly Tony Meade's "luck" happened on his very next trip and, together with his crew, they added to our list of losses on these patrols.

Meanwhile another crew borrowed our own favourite Whitley "S for Sugar." We never learned what happened, the bomber flew down the Bay on a sortie early one morning and never returned. This explains why the registration number of the replacement "S" Sugar Whitley does not appear in my log book, I was tardy in making a note of it, and events overtook me before I could do so.

From the heights of the fame of flying with the Squadron commander I was brought back to earth with a bump when detailed for two flights with a couple of the latest intake pilots. The first was to test the gunners efficiency in firing at towed drogue targets and the second, which threatened to be a tedious cross-country exercise, had to be cut short when I reported one of the main generators faulty.

Although replacement new aircraft had been arriving to make up our losses there were insufficient crews to fly them. On September 16th I acted as tail gunner on two flights to St Eval from where we took back with us to Chivenor twenty aircrew, a mixed bag of pilots, navigators, wireless operators and gunners. They were not very happy, having had high hopes of being posted to one of the up-and-coming new four-engined squadrons.

At this time Bartlett had influenza so "Pop" Acree took over as boss of our crew. Flying in "X – X-Ray" on September 18th we were given the French inshore patrol. Everything was peaceful and we had no alarms, although a late takeoff meant a night landing during an air raid alert.

Then, as far as I was concerned came a quiet few days. Apart from "Pop" and myself trying out the new "S" in practice descents through low cloud (QGH) there was little to do other than look forward to my next leave which was due at the end of the month.

I liked "Pop" very much. Originally with a Wellington squadron he was, perhaps, not as polished as Bartlett in his handling of a Whitley, but he was totally reliable and I never saw his even temperament ruffled. The last exercise we did together had its dangers, coming down through low cloud when the ground did not become visible until below five hundred feet could be a tense affair, but he never doubted the information gleaned from the base ground station which I passed to him. This was our last flight together and I never knew what happened to him, whether he survived the war or not.

CHAPTER 7

Search Mission and Disaster

September 24th was a fine, warm sunny morning. We were stood down that day and I was chatting to the ground crew outside the Flight Office when Operations telephoned to ask if a crew could be quickly organised to search for an aircraft dinghy, possibly with survivors on board, which had been reported drifting in the Bristol Channel somewhere between Lundy and Cardiff.

Outside the Flight Office the only aircrew were Flight Lieutenant Parker, one of the squadron's most skilful and experienced pilots, and two members of Bartlett's crew, the other WOP/AG and myself. Whilst a Whitley could be flown locally with just a crew of three there was the danger of being intercepted over the Bristol Channel by German aircraft. It was therefore imperative that the rear guns were manned and, even more importantly, if the dinghy and survivors were sighted two additional crewmen would be needed to drop survival kit to them.

As Flight Lieutenant Parker started up the engines of "W – William" I leaned out of the fuselage door and yelled for two volunteers from the ground crew to help us. Great blokes that they were I think they would all have come, as it was the Corporal Fitter and Corporal Armourer were the two who grabbed Mae Wests and clambered on board. One of the Corporals was named Todd and came from Leeds, the other was an Irish boy whose name I can no longer remember.

We took off and began a low level search, starting at a Hartland Point – Tenby crisscross of the water and gradually working our way eastwards up the Channel. That morning the sea was calm and although there was a slight haze visibility was reasonably good.

In the cockpit with the pilot were the two corporals, one sitting in the copilot's seat and the other the navigator's. My fellow sergeant was behind the radio equipment whilst I was acting as rear gunner. That suited me fine as I not only felt safer than if anyone else had been watching the tail but I could also smoke a cigarette or two.

Airborne just over two hours without seeing any trace of a dinghy we were about ten miles south of Swansea when, to my dismay a cloud of white smoke suddenly began to stream down the port side of the aircraft past my turret. Trying to keep my voice steady I spoke into my microphone : "Skipper, we have a glycol leak in the port engine."

Glycol was the coolant fluid for the Rolls Royce Merlin engines which powered the Whitley VI. White smoke meant that there was a rupture in the coolant lines and the glycol fluid was leaking away. As the engine overheated the white smoke would quickly turn to dense black and the engine would burst into flames. Then you really had trouble.

In response to my report came a laconic "Thank you. Feathering port engine now."

This he did and as the propeller stopped the smoke diminished. But there were still problems. The search pattern we had been following meant that our height was only about 1500 feet, not much margin for error, flying on one engine and struggling to maintain altitude, let alone climb.

My unsort-for opinion was to put the aircraft down in the Channel and hope the Air Sea Rescue services would find us. Unfortunately Flight Lieutenant Parker had been forced to "ditch" a Whitley whilst on a Bay of Biscay patrol three weeks earlier. Although he and his crew were picked up by a launch from Penzance after only six hours he had no desire to repeat the experience.

"Get me a course for base," he instructed, "we'll try and make it back to Chivenor."

Search Mission and Disaster

Maybe it would have been better if we had simply crossed to the Devon side of the Channel and followed the coast round to Morte Bay, after where we had a direct approach across the Taw estuary to Chivenor without having to cross any high ground. That is merely supposition. The pilot, as I have already said, was one of the squadron's best. As calm as always he gave no hint of the struggle he was having to keep the Whitley in the air. No doubt his judgement to return to Chivenor in the shortest possible time, by the shortest route, was correct and the shortest distance between two points is in a straight line.

A few choice words over the intercom prodded our friend acting as wireless operator to forget his fascination with the feathered port propeller and ask base for an emergency QDM (What is my course to steer with zero wind to reach you?). Through my earphones I could hear the stammer of answering Chivenor Morse giving the information requested and asking us what was our problem?

Crossing the coast somewhere between Lynton and Porlock we began to struggle up the Doone Valley. Ahead of us threatened the high ground of Exmoor. We wriggled round the highest points by following the minor road which climbs up from Simonsbath, but by now our one good engine, the starboard, was beginning to overheat and backfire.

The intercom crackled : "It's no good," said Parker, "we can't make it. Sorry, but I'll have to put her down as best I can. Crash positions everybody."

I clambered out of the rear turret and, as instructed in so many training sessions, clambered forward to the bomb bay step which was about halfway up the fuselage. From here I could see both the corporals sitting in the cockpit with the pilot. They looked calm enough, but their only response to my signals for them to come back and join me in the crash position was a negative shaking of their heads. I don't remember, at this stage seeing our wireless operator.

"Hold tight," came the unruffled voice of the pilot, "there's a field ahead. We're going in."

I sat down on the bomb bay step, facing rearwards, grabbing one of the aluminium fuselage ribs with my left hand and the Beam Approach aerial with my right. Looking down the aircraft through the open doors of the turret I had just vacated I could see a line of trees and the green grass of a field. As we hit there was an awful juddering sensation and a cacophony of indescribable screeching.

Suddenly, everything was silent.

For a moment I imagined I was dead.

Then I heard the sounds of birds squawking and opened my eyes.

I was lying on my back, but still in the Whitley. Both my hands were bleeding, I had gripped my supports so tightly. My battledress was torn and I had a bloody right knee sticking out of my trousers. Perhaps I would have lain there for ever, but suddenly a voice shouted : "For Christ's sake, is there any one in there?"

That got me moving. "Fire!" I thought. "The bloody thing's going to blow up!"

The tail gun turret was half-split away from the fuselage, and by my side was a hole in the side of the Whitley which previously had been the rear door. Behind me, where should have been the front half of the bomber, there was nothing at all. As I began to try and scramble through the hole badly needed help came in the form of the young man I had heard shouting.

"Get away," I said, "there could be a fire any second."

"Come on then," came the reply, "put your arm round my shoulder and let's get moving."

He half-dragged, half-carried me away from the wreck. Then lowering me to the ground and ignoring the possibility of explosion and fire, went back again to what had been "W – William."

From halfway along the fuselage back to the twin rudders the Whitley was more or less intact. Forward of this section, separated by a distance of some thirty feet, was an

Search Mission and Disaster

unrecognisable tangled mass of metal. Incredibly, out of this crawled the wireless operator, badly hurt – but alive.

It was almost exactly forty years later to the day when, in 1982, I returned to the scene and learned for the first time what had happened.

As the Whitley laboured over the last high ground of Exmoor the one remaining engine was rapidly losing the power to keep her airborne. Although, by now, only ten miles from Chivenor, it was obviously impossible to get there. Seeing what appeared to be reasonably flat farm land ahead Flight Lieutenant Parker warned the crew of an imminent wheels-up crash landing. Excellent pilot that he was, under the circumstances the touchdown was perfect. But as in most things, as well as skill, there has to be an element of luck.

His was bad.

The field in which he landed seemed to be divided from the adjacent one by a hedge. The hedge was there alright, but what it concealed was a sunken road, so typical of that part of the country.

Sliding across the ground, still at a speed of about ninety miles per hour, the bomber went nose down into the lane, totally destroying the aircraft as far back as the cockpit and ripping off the engines and wings, thus minimising the risk of fire. The rear half of the Whitley, with me inside it, rolled over and over before coming to rest almost in a farmyard.

The Prudhoe family at North Horridge farm, Stoke Rivers, were just finishing their midday meal when unexpected visitors dropped in on them. Suddenly the peaceful quiet of their world was shattered by the roaring of an aircraft engine, followed immediately by a series of ear-splitting crashes rising to a crescendo as the stricken aircraft disintegrated.

It was the son of the family, then in his mid-twenties, who dashed out of the farmhouse kitchen and dragged me clear. I have only hazy memories of what followed. I can recall lying on my back in the field whilst the Prudhoes sought in vain to find any other survivors, Flight Lieutenant Parker and the two corporals had been killed instantly.

I was carried carefully into the kitchen and sat in a chair whilst the son's mother, Mrs Prudhoe aided, I think, by the local vicar's wife, gave me first aid. The Stoke Rivers telephone lines had been severed by the crashing Whitley and some frantic cycling by a member of the Home Guard to the next village was necessary before more help could be summoned. When ambulances finally arrived my fellow survivor, the other WOP/AG was fully conscious but terrified that the dead bodies might be put in the same vehicle as ourselves. They gave him an injection which calmed him down, and I was more than thankful for a sip of tea and a cigarette.

A long, long time has now gone by, but I have never forgotten the courage and kindness of the Prudhoe family and all the others in the area who came to help.

I have been back to Stoke Rivers just once. That was in September 1982 when, together with my second wife Marjorie, I called at North Horridge farm. The Prudhoe family still lived there, three generations of them. The Grandfather who, like myself, had grown old, had been the young man who pulled me out of the Whitley. He recognised me immediately.

"Sergeant Goodwin," he exclaimed. "Wonderful to see you!"

It was wonderful to be there.

CHAPTER 8

Respite – for a while

My physical injuries were slight. Although I was being well looked after in the civilian hospital at Barnstaple I was extremely anxious to get back to Chivenor and go home on the seven days leave which was due to me. Bill Dudgeon and Sid Hodges my closest friends on the squadron, smuggled into the hospital a spare uniform. After an argument with the Ward Sister I succeeded in discharging myself and, painful though it was limped and hitched my way back to the airfield, some five miles away. There, a sympathetic Medical Officer, ensured that I was issued with the necessary paperwork and travel documents, and home I went.

Nora was in the third month of her pregnancy. 1942 was not the best of times to be having a baby, especially when the husband was operational aircrew. Rightly so, she was very concerned, and the war news, which at this stage seemed to grow worse every day, did nothing to help.

I had only been at home two days when a telegram came recalling me to the squadron. However, my hands had begun to tremble so much I could not lift a cup of tea, or worse still a glass of beer, to my mouth without spilling most of it. The Medical Officer at RAF Wilmslow diagnosed delayed shock and instead of returning to Chivenor I was given extended leave. One day we went back to Blackpool and, hopefully, in the photographs which I am including with this missive, is one of Nora and myself walking on the Promenade. She was twenty-one and I was twenty-two years old.

Nora and I: Blackpool 1942

On my return to duty I found myself submitted to all sorts of medical and psychological tests to determine whether or not I was fit enough to do the job for which I had been trained. When asked if I still wanted to continue flying I answered truthfully that I certainly was not unduly concerned at the thought of never getting into an aircraft again. This led to much clicking of tongues and shaking of heads, but no one made an issue of it.

Unfortunately, or maybe fortunately – I will never know which – so far as I was concerned the then situation became very confused. 51 squadron was stood down from the Bay of Biscay daylight sweeps and transferred back to Bomber Command. This meant the unit leaving Chivenor and moving to Snaith, an airfield located just outside Goole. Here four-engined Halifaxes were to replace the old Whitleys, those that were left! No one had any time to waste on an old has-been like myself and most of the time, for the next few weeks, I was

Respite – for a while

a lone figure in the Sergeant's Mess. Both Sid and Bill were away at another airfield, Marston Moor in Yorkshire, on conversion courses to the Halifax and, as the others there were all replacement intake, there was not one familiar face. I did not know anyone and, worse still, nobody knew me.

One day, in desperation, I "borrowed" an RAF bicycle which some careless person had left outside the Officer's Mess. It was an ancient "sit up and beg" model, no gears and a fixed wheel, that is you were unable to "free wheel" but applying backward pressure on the pedals certainly helped to brake the contraption, always providing you were not catapulted over the handlebars.

Having wobbled my way round the perimeter track I decided to venture into the great wide world outside. The guards on the gate waved me through without a question, no doubt slightly amazed that, at last, one of the indolent, scruffy aircrew types was making an effort to keep fit.

Outside the camp ran the main road from Goole to Knottingley and from there to Wakefield and Denby Dale through Holmfirth, then, over the Pennines to Hyde and Stockport. Something like sixty miles, possibly, I reckoned, and I could be home. To a pre-war keen cyclist like myself sixty miles was nothing. Of course in those days I had a lightweight three-speed Sun cycle, not a lump of iron like the one I was riding now. I decided that the difference was not all that important, and the fact that I was wearing uniform, heavy in comparison to the clothes worn on my earlier two-wheeled adventures, never entered my head.

Clear of the camp, no one coming after me and nothing else to do, I might as well go. I did.

When I left Snaith it would be about two in the afternoon. By the time I reached Wakefield I was tiring and it was beginning to go dark. Then I realised that my bicycle had no lights. As I was more confident of the way ahead of me than trying to return to Snaith I kept going. Although, most of the time, obscured by clouds the moon gave sufficient illumination for me to see the road in front. There were no lights, and no direction signs either. The latter had all been removed to prevent any enemy who may land knowing where they were. Whether that was effective I don't know, but it certainly confused the British.

After what seemed an eternity I reached Holmfirth, a town shrouded in its blackout, and without a sign of life – not even a dog barked as I laboriously pedalled my panting way through. If the going so far had been hard it now became absolute torture. The gradual uphill climb from Wakefield was replaced by the horrendous slopes of the road which would take me to the summit. I think I walked most of that stretch, only the thought of a blessed downhill ride on the other side kept me going. Eventually the road levelled out and I was able to place my saddle-sore posterior once again on the bike and begin the descent. Of course I had forgotten that the contraption had a fixed-wheel and my envisaged gloriously energy-free glide of the next six miles or so down to Oldham and civilisation became a nightmare of screeching round bends desperately trying to keep my feet on the pedals and trying to slow down the speed. The brakes, I now discovered, did little or nothing to help.

By some miracle, I arrived in Oldham. All night I had seen no other traffic of any kind on the road. Now there was a glimmer of light in the sky with the approaching dawn and the cheerful sound of a milkman on his morning round. I was absolutely exhausted, but the thought of home less than twenty miles away drove me on. I arrived there in time for breakfast, after which I spent the next twenty-four hours in a deep, untroubled sleep from which, apart from walking like a cowboy who had just ridden an extremely difficult horse, I awoke almost as good as new. It had taken me eighteen hours to cycle from the airfield at Snaith to my home in Cheshire. I could have walked it in the time.

There was no knock on the door from the Military Police asking for my whereabouts, but nevertheless I began to worry about being absent without leave from an operational unit. There was no way I was going to attempt the cycle ride back to Snaith, but someone, most likely Mother, bought rail tickets for the pair of us, so after three days more there was a tearful farewell as together with my trusty steed in the luggage van the train from Poynton took us on our way.

I rode up to the main gate at Snaith expecting to immediately be placed under arrest. Instead the Sergeant in charge smiled affably and asked me if I had enjoyed the ride. I hadn't, but he expected me to say yes, so I did.

My room was exactly as I had left it, there were no orders waiting for me and, obviously, I hadn't been missed. I found myself a little distressed about that. It is always nice to be wanted.

Along came December and training intensified as the squadron worked up to operational standard. A new Commanding Officer arrived, full of enthusiasm and determined to make 51 squadron the ace outfit in Number Four Group, Bomber Command. One of the first things he did was to clear out the dead wood, and that included me. One morning I was called to the Orderly Room and given an envelope which contained a rail voucher and orders to report to RAF Uxbridge. I was not very happy. Nothing I had heard about Uxbridge inspired confidence. It had the reputation of being the strictest disciplinarian unit in the service. I asked for an interview with the new CO and had it been granted would have expressed my fervent desire to carry on flying. The request was turned down flat, apparently, so far as he was concerned, to express doubt just the once meant that he would never ever trust you. He may have been right, but there is little doubt that his intransigent mentality was an important factor in my surviving the war.

Down to Uxbridge I went and, to my surprise, was given a friendly reception and allocated a very pleasant room. The following morning four officers discussed with me my past and, my future. Two wore the insignia of the medical profession, the others were high-ranking and much decorated pilots. I assumed, rightly, that the papers they each had in front of them gave details of my RAF career so far. They seemed to be reasonably impressed, and expressed regret that

I could not see my way to continue. Still in view of my experiences at Chivenor, and the fact that my wife was expecting a baby in four months time, they could quite understand my reluctance to carry on as aircrew. I must, however, realise that if I stood down from flying then I would lose my non-substantive rank of sergeant. Pity really, did I mind? Of course I didn't. Good then, that's decided, but would I please keep the stripes on my arm for a while yet as Uxbridge was desperately short of Orderly Sergeants. I agreed and left the room with handshakes and their grateful thanks. A funny war.

For three months, every other day, I did my stint as Uxbridge Orderly Sergeant. The early morning parades were the worst part of the job, especially marching the sick, the lame and the lazy down to the medical centre. To my horror I developed toothache myself but, having listened to the howls of pain from those unfortunates I took to the dental trainee unit on the camp, I went outside into the town and paid for an extraction at a private dentist.

Uxbridge was an interesting experience, various sections of the peacetime constructed base fulfilling many different functions, most of which were completely unknown, not only to the general public, but also to the vast majority of RAF personnel. There were several aircrew cast-offs like myself awaiting either discharge or direction into another trade. Among them were two survivors from a crash in the Western Desert of North Africa, who had taken several days to crawl back to friendly territory and could not be trusted to pass a tap without turning it full on and laughing insanely as the water gushed forth. Then there was Sergeant Bill Brown, who I had known slightly at Kinloss. He was classified as an "evader," that is, shot down over enemy territory but contriving to return to the UK without being caught by the Germans or their friends. He had been the wireless operator of a raiding Halifax which was attacked by a night fighter and burst into flames. After clipping on his own parachute he then tried to assist the pilot to secure his pack. The pilot's name was Tippits-Aylmer, a bit of a daredevil, with whom I had flown once the previous April. He was fighting hard to keep the burning Halifax straight and level while as many as possible of the surviving crew abandoned the aircraft. Bill was forced to turn away and leave his skipper to his fate. He landed safely and within minutes was located and hustled into hiding by members of the Dutch Resistance. Two months later, after being passed from one unit to another along an established escape chain, he reached Spain, then Gibraltar and home, or the nearest thing to it – Uxbridge. His parents were informed of his safety but he was confined to the limits of the camp for an indeterminate period, not allowed any leave, or even telephone calls. He was allowed to write letters providing they were subjected to censorship. All this was a precaution to prevent him telling the story of his escape and unwittingly compromise the Dutch Resistance organisation before they had been able to re-arrange their rendezvous and couriers.

Home for Christmas was, of course, impossible. An emotional time, I found myself missing life on the squadron, especially Sid and Bill, with whom I had completely lost touch. In a sombre mood I spent several hours on Christmas Eve in bars and clubs in central London with the idea of finding myself a nice girl or, if needs be, a prostitute. I found neither but had a sore head Christmas morning.

The end of January, a posting to a signals station near Reading, and the loss of my three stripes. I hardly settled in my comfortable billet with an elderly lady when orders came for me to transfer to a secret communications centre at Altrincham. Within cycling distance of Poynton I was able to arrange to be billeted in my own home, and Nora's mother was very pleased to have the ration allowances for me!

Of course, it was too good to last. Came March 1943, and I was called to the War Office in London for an interview by an army Major. He gave me no clues as to what it was all about, but I was to find out in due course. Meanwhile I was to learn that Sid Hodges and Bill Dudgeon had been killed over Germany.

April fifth, and my son Bryan was born. A few days later along came another telegram telling me to report to West Kirby in the Wirral. I knew what that presaged – I was going overseas. Just as she had arranged our wedding fifteen months previously, Nora hastily organised for Bryan to be christened at Poynton church, and the following morning I was on my way.

CHAPTER 9

North Africa

Three days at the West Kirby camp, then the short journey by lorry to Liverpool docks and on to the troopship. She was the "Duchess of York," in peacetime a Canadian Pacific liner of some 22,000 tons. Luxury cruise liner she may have been pre-war, but in 1943 all her cabins slept at least eight people instead of two and the vast bulk of her lower decks and holds had been stripped to accommodate hundreds of servicemen. Those unfortunate people, and I was one of them, slept, or tried to sleep, in hammocks which were crammed close to each other and as the ship rolled in rough weather swung in unison to the groans of the seasick and the weary. There was no natural light, all portholes above the water line had been sealed, and at meal times food was brought down in large dixies from whence it was ladled out into the mess tins of those who were able to face it.

Sailing from Liverpool we met up with other troopships when off the Firth of Clyde. The "Duchess of York" was in the centre of the convoy which was escorted by destroyers, one battle cruiser and an aircraft carrier. I used to watch the Swordfish 'planes taking off and landing on the heaving deck of the carrier and marvel at the courage of the men who flew them. The old "Stringbags" (as they were known) made the late lamented Whitleys seem ultramodern by comparison. From time to time there were extra flurries of activity as single or several U-boats were either located, or suspected, in the vicinity.

The voyage lasted twelve days. For the first week we could only guess at our eventual destination as we first sailed northwards towards Iceland, then to the west almost to

Newfoundland, and finally at high speed back across the Atlantic to the Straits of Gibraltar. Here our escort was strengthened even more as we proceeded along the coast of North Africa before being put ashore at Algiers. It was good to be back on dry land. Conditions on board a troopship were always grim. At night lying in a swaying hammock, fastened together with a hundred others in your own particular deck space, and waiting fearfully for the next thump on the ship's hull as one of the destroyers depth charged a U-boat (real or otherwise) was not conducive to a restful night. It was much better in daylight, even when the alarms sounded for possible submarine or air attack. Then, although sometimes kept for hours at our lifeboat stations, there did seem a chance of survival if anything went wrong. The "Duchess of York" suffered neither direct attack nor damage in this particular convoy, but we heard later that she was bombed and hit on the return journey to the United Kingdom.

Algeria had been successfully invaded by American and British troops a while before our arrival. Based in tents at the Algiers racecourse we were able to walk into the city which was quite attractive, and sit drinking coffee or one of the local wines, mainly muscatel. The latter was cheap, and plentiful but many of the British discovered that over indulgence, allied to the hot sunshine meant a night spent admiring the scenery from a perch on one of the poles running over a trench which served as a latrine.

Security round the racecourse was very tight, armed sentries being on constant patrol. To get out into the city a pass had to be shown at the main gate, the pass being in the form of a packet of French Letters, better known today as condoms. These were issued free by the medical orderlies, who also ran a nice little racket in selling names and addresses where they could be put to the best use. On returning to the camp the packet had to be shown to the guards before admittance was granted. If the packet could not be shown, in which case it was assumed that the contents had been used, then the main gate was barred to the returning soldier or airman. He had to report to a special side entrance where he was immediately seized by enthusiastic specially trained VD experts. The treatment they meted out to the embarrassed lover was talked about in hushed breath by the others. Personally, I refused to believe half of it, I considered it to be physically impossible.

However, most of us clung to our issued contraceptives as if they were packets of gold. If they could not be produced on demand then it was off to the torture chambers. There was one unfortunate soul who refused to have any part of it. He was a staunch Roman Catholic and did not believe in any form of birth control. One day he somehow got out of the camp and went down into the city where he had a pleasant afternoon, his nearest approach to libation being a second cup of coffee. Returning to the racecourse camp was a disaster. The Service Police were totally unmoved by his stern lecture on the sins of promiscuous sex and did not believe he could possibly have got out of the camp without his condoms. So where were they now? He had not got them. Q.E.D. it was the side gate and the *treatment*. The poor lad was heartbroken and came back to his tent sobbing his heart out. All we could suggest was that he sought out the Chaplain of his faith and confess his sins. "But I haven't done anything to confess," he cried. "If not in deed, perhaps in thought," we said. It was the best part of a week before he spoke to us again.

We were not beloved by the local French populace either, they found it very hard to forgive the British for the attack of two years ago on their fleet based just along the coast at Oran. Although there was no active hostility it was impossible to make friends with any of them.

There came the day when I was told to report to the conglomeration of large tents which served as the RAF Headquarters for Algeria. Here, to my surprise, I was issued with a Sten gun and three clips of ammunition. I then discovered the reason for a long-ago interview in London with an army Major. I was attached as RAF signals liaison to the 1st Airborne Division.

I reached my new destination, after an eventful journey from Algiers by rail in an open wagon to a town named Mascara. Eventful because in the blazing sun I had to sit on my kitbag clutching my loaded Sten and keeping a wary eye open for marauding Arabs who had a habit of creeping up to stationary trains, and they were stationary quite often, and with an adept quick slice with a knife would empty packed parcels and kitbags within seconds. I was nearly caught out once when a little urchin appeared at one side of the track offering two boiled eggs or the services of his sister at an extremely reasonable price. I was just about to negotiate (for the boiled eggs, of course) when instinct made me turn round. There, on the other side of my wagon was an elder brother, knife at the ready, about to get to work on my kitbag. The clicking of the Sten gun's safety catch and they were both away.

At Mascara I found an American Jeep waiting for me. The driver, a good-natured Top Sergeant from Texas welcomed me to the Airborne's depot. He informed me that as well as the British Airborne Division, "the Yanks" (his words) were also there in large numbers. They were flying Waco gliders, about half the size of the Horsa, and all operations henceforth were to be undertaken together. All this on the short drive to the tents and airfield which made up the Mascara base.

Reporting to the powers-that-be I was made welcome and told to acclimatise myself as quickly as possible. Things, apparently, were about to happen.

My records had reached them the day before and, understandably, caused some amusement, especially to a much be-ribboned American Major who sat in the tent with his feet on a table using the contents of a can of beer to alleviate the hot dusty atmosphere.

I had been unfit for flying in bombers. If this caused the Air Force any problem as to my further use to them they solved it in their own inimitable way, the Airborne unit to which I was attached flew in Horsa gliders. Towed by either the four-engined Halifax, or occasionally the less powerful twin-engined Albermarle, the Horsa was a large all-wooden glider which carried up to thirty soldiers, fully armed and equipped, and still had room for a light field gun or antitank gun. After being used to the noise of bomber engines I found, at first, the almost silent glider unnerving, especially after the towing aircraft cast off the connecting cable and the Horsa, with flaps extended, dived steeply to the designated landing spot with the wind sighing past the fuselage.

Horsa Glider

On the northern edge of the Sahara desert the airstrip, named Froha, was located only a mile or so outside the small town of Mascara, making it possible to walk there during off-duty spells. I found it possible to carry out a reasonable conversation with the local Arabs in my schoolboy French, but the French members of the population either could not, or perhaps would not, understand a word I said. We spent two weeks in this area, time put to good use in getting used to the climate and the Horsa gliders. Then came the order to get back into the war.

The campaign in North Africa was over. American troops, together with the British First Army had finally linked up with the Eighth Army (the Desert Rats) and the German Afrika

Corps, or what was left of it, surrendered. During our brief stay in Algiers we had watched the columns of prisoners as they marched to the docks and the ships which would take them into captivity. They had tramped for hundreds of miles along hot dusty tracks and roads yet their formations were impeccable and their heads were held high. Their departure from the scene meant the Allies had, for the first time in the war, control of the whole of the North African coastline. The way was now open for an invasion of southern Europe, and the unit to which I was attached was assigned a vital role.

From Mascara we were moved to an airstrip which had been originally laid down by the Luftwaffe. British Engineers had made some improvements, mainly by laying down special matting over the sand to cope with the Halifax bombers and the heavily laden Horsa gliders. The base went under the glamorous name of Kairouan "F" Strip and was sited in the desert approximately twenty miles inland from Sfax and Sousse in the Gulf of Gabes. The flight from Mascara to "F" Strip was an experience in itself. Towed by Halifax bombers the Horsas had to cross the Atlas mountains to reach the Tunisian base. Clad only in shorts and shirts as the gliders rose from the heat of the desert the cold became so excruciating that stomach cramp was quickly followed in many cases by severe diarrhoea. The glider had no toilet facilities on board so the only solution was to use the large dixies, in which we prepared our meals, and as they filled up empty them through the fuselage door. This was a rather hazardous procedure in more ways than one with an air speed of over one hundred and fifty miles per hour. Although the dixie-emptier was prevented from falling out by fellow passengers literally hanging on to his shirt-tails, slipstream can play some funny tricks. From time to time, instead of the dixie's contents streaming clear astern, they came back to splatter those in range of the door. After we landed the only way to clean out the dixies was with sand – water was too precious to use.

CHAPTER 10

"F Strip" and Sicily

Our new base at Kairouan turned out to be very hot and uncomfortable. Not very far away were the Great Salt lakes of Tunisia and when the wind blew from that direction, which it did most of the time, in addition to the dry heat salt and sand got into our eyes, ears and food. To drink, wash and shave we were rationed to a half pint of water per day. This was carefully poured into our service issue canteen every morning. We never bothered to launder any clothing, all we wore were shirts, shorts, gaiters (no socks) and boots. We were free from lice, probably too hot for them, scorpions were the biggest danger.

Everyone at the airstrip, Army or RAF, officers and other ranks, had the same accommodation, "pup" tents. These were tents, about six feet long and three feet high and wide, which would accommodate one man and his kit. Not exactly the lap of luxury. Terribly hot and cramped during the day, but even worse at night when the temperature dropped quickly within an hour from 35°C (100°F) down to 10°C (50°F). This sudden change caused cases of pneumonia amongst those who did not pull out sweaters, or other extra clothing, from their kitbags.

In addition to myself there was one other RAF wireless operator. His name was Smith and he came from Bolton in Lancashire. Between us we had to keep open a link, through Gibraltar, with the United Kingdom as well as with Tripoli, Tunis and Algiers. We worked a twenty-four hour day, one resting whilst the other was on watch. Smith or I had to pay particular attention to one frequency (or channel) at specified times. We suspected, but were never told, that this might be an agent working just across the water in enemy occupied Sicily. Providing we were always on the alert we were left to carry on with the job. We were fully occupied, as well as transmitting and receiving messages in Morse we had also the responsibility of coding and decoding.

We were soon joined at Kairouan by units of the American Airborne Division. They came in their own gliders, the Wacos, which were fabric covered and only half the size of our Horsas. Towed by Dakotas, to us the gliders were aptly named. If, on takeoff, the glider pilot did not correctly time his pull-off from the ground to the exact second, the slipstream from the Dakota had an unfortunate habit of turning the Waco upside down. Sometimes the resultant crash was funny, as troops and equipment frantically clawed their way out of the wreckage, but all too often someone was seriously injured and occasionally lives were lost.

Whatever the consequences, however, training for the forthcoming invasion of southern Europe continued unabated. Brought in by air, "F" Strip was now well stocked-up with ammunition and fuel. All the aircraft had to be refuelled by hand, from the cans of petrol so transported, a long and tedious job. The full cans of fuel were stored in a ring of about 100 yards diameter, one can on top of another. The centre of the ring was kept hollow, *for it was here that the guards were quartered !* During the day the heat expanded the fuel drums, which didn't create any problems. In the evening, when the temperature dropped, the drums contracted. The result was a series of tinny bangs which went on for hours. Nervous sentries could be heard challenging non-existent enemy intruders whilst the rest of the base fervently prayed that some trigger-happy soldier would not open fire and blow the place to smithereens.

Only on one occasion was there a genuine emergency. That was when enemy aircraft came over and parachutists were dropped around us. It looked as if it was going to be a case of the biter being bit, but the descending foe turned out to be Italians who promptly surrendered.

At the time I happened to be on duty. Earlier that day I had contrived to get six cans of beer from one of the transport aircrew. I had these with me in the operations tent, intending to barter them with an American for cigarettes. As reports of the descending parachutists came in from our outposts I decided that it would not be very loyal to allow the enemy to capture my ale. I had just opened the first can and was about to drink it when the Operations Officer rushed in and shouted "We are under attack – radio for reinforcements – my God ! – Drinking on duty – you are on a charge !" That was all in one breath, the man thoroughly deserved the medal he was later to earn. However, the panic soon subsided, some two hundred happy Italian prisoners were brought in, and I never heard any more about drinking on duty.

It may have been in the excitement here, or it could have been in several incidents earlier, including the air crash in Devon, but somewhere along the way I lost a cigarette case. This had been given to me by Nora's mother, I think it was silver, held ten cigarettes and had an inscription giving the name of John Mountfort, and a New Zealand army service number. Originally the case had been left behind in England by a New Zealand soldier, John Mountfort who, whilst on leave from the Western Front in 1916, visited his relatives and the farm from which he had emigrated six years earlier.

I always carried the case as a good luck token in the breast pocket of my battle dress, but my memory totally fails me as to when I lost it.

However, many years later, in Woodville, New Zealand, a son of John Mountfort, also named John, had the surprise of his life when, through the post, arrived his father's cigarette case. Someone, somewhere, had found it, handed it in to the army authorities who, with the assistance of New Zealand House and the inscribed service number, had traced the family of the original owner.

Although by the end of June I had only been in Tunisia for a few weeks I began to worry about the situation back home. I had left Nora with a very young baby whose health was causing some concern. Hopefully, everything would be alright, but I had no way of knowing and there had been no personal mail from the UK reaching Kairouan as yet. If Nora had received any letters from me there would be no indication as to where I actually was, apart from a serial number under the heading British North African Air Force. Not a happy state of affairs as far as I was concerned.

One day, coding up messages for the Gibraltar contact for relay to the UK I had the bright idea of slipping in one of my own. It requested a report on the state of health and wellbeing of a certain Mrs Goodwin and child, this information was urgently required and essential to the wellbeing of her husband. The signal was sent in that evening's transmissions and I sat back and waited results.

I was not too worried about any repercussions from a discovery of my unauthorised signal. To begin with, the chances of that happening I had previously calculated as being slim and, if it were found out, apart from a severe dressing down virtually nothing else could be done. Loss of pay or leave were both inconsequential whilst I was at "F" strip.

Nothing whatever happened – nothing at all. Not in Tunisia. The illegality of my message was not reported. But back in England, as I was to discover months later, there had been repercussions.

One day, much to the alarm of my wife, a high-ranking officer alighted from a large car, driven by a Waaf corporal, which had drawn up outside our home. He was kindness personified, after putting her mind at rest regarding the continued existence of her gallant warrior husband fighting the foe he knew where, but was not allowed to tell her, he wanted to know how our child was faring and if all was well why didn't she write to the aforementioned husband and tell him so. When assured she was writing to her spouse at the only address she had nearly every day, and so far, in return, had not received one letter herself the officer shook his head sadly. "Nothing is like it used to be," he said, "not even the post. I will see what I can do about it."

I never knew who he was, or which particular section of the RAF he presented, but he was a very kind man. As he left he handed my wife, "for the nipper" a five pound note (a small fortune in those days) wished her well and told her not to worry.

That is not quite the end of the story. The finale was to come quite some time afterwards.

Back in Tunisia. By the beginning of July, 1943, everything was ready and in position for the invasion of Sicily. At Kairouan the British Airborne were briefed to capture the road bridge at Syracuse, and to hold it until the forces being landed by sea could reach them. The Americans had a similar job to do at Catania, which was said to be the easier proposition of the two. The British considered themselves to be unlucky, but events proved otherwise. Somewhere in the planning naval forces had not been informed of the American's flight path to Catania. In the dark night, flying at low altitude, and towed by the slow Dakotas, the Wacos, with their heavily laden troops and equipment were subjected to fierce anti-aircraft fire by Allied surface craft. Many of the gliders were shot down into the sea with heavy loss of life. The Syracuse operation went like clockwork and casualties were light.

After the departure of the last of the gliders and their troops "F" strip was unnaturally quiet. The aircrews and ground staff sat around in whatever shelter from the sun they could find, smoking, playing cards and hoping the war had not passed on leaving them stranded in the wilderness for ever. One day the boredom was eased when the Americans organised a fleet of lorries and took everyone down to the coast at Sousse. Here we wallowed in the warm Mediterranean, washing off the weeks of dust and dirt whilst some local Arab women made a small fortune laundering every item of clothing we would give them. They did not seem to be impressed by the sight of a hundred or so naked men frolicking in the sea or sitting on the beach eating succulent juicy melons.

Cleansed and dressed again in clean shorts and shirt I joined a queue outside a house which I had been told was a newly opened Naafi canteen where for a modest few francs one could obtain a good cup of tea and that much sought-after luxury, the good old British rock bun. The vital information I lacked was that the canteen was downstairs and the queue for that was at a rear door to the house. I tagged on to a lengthy column outside the front door and paid the five francs demanded. Eventually I was admitted and on climbing the stairs found myself in a brothel with a demonstration performance in one room and, for a further five francs allowed to join another queue outside that bedroom door waiting for the delectable services of one of the two girls operating in there. I went to the demonstration and learned that, given the will and the right equipment, nothing in sex is impossible. Tea and a rock bun would have been far more enjoyable.

The invasion of Sicily was going well and by now ground forces had linked up with Airborne troops. That meant the end of their involvement in this stage of the proceedings and with it, Smith's and my own association with them. We were politely thanked and told to find our own way back to the UK by any means we could. As the surviving Halifax tugs were also making their way back home it was not too difficult to arrange a lift in one of them. So, on July 18th I shook the sand of Kairouan off my boots for the last time as "Q" Queenie took off for Ras el Ma in French Morocco. Here the aircraft's engines required attention which gave me the opportunity to go into the town and buy a canister of grapes to take home. This was the last time I saw my fellow wireless operator Smith from "F" strip, he too was flying home in another Halifax. Both 'planes took off for home on the morning of July 20th, initially in good flying conditions. As we flew northwards the weather deteriorated alarmingly and my pilot, Flight Lieutenant Grant, wisely decided to return to Ras el Ma. Disappointing as this was when we were so looking forward to going home it was the right thing to do. The aircraft with Smith on board continued on, only to disappear and never be heard of again.

Two days later we tried again this time successfully, although not without some concern. As we came up the Bay of Biscay one engine failed and we, once again ran into low cloud and bad weather. Our estimated time of arrival at St. Eval in Cornwall came and went and there was no sign of land. A second engine then failed. Just as it seemed we were destined for serious trouble came the welcome sight of waves breaking at the foot of cliffs – not Cornwall as we at first thought – but Anglesey!

Still, there's a saying that every landing you walk away from is a good one, and this was certainly that. The airfield turned out to be that of Valley, not far from Holyhead. I was a bit of a problem to the Commanding Officer there as all my kit had gone astray in the excitement of the Sicily invasion. I had no uniform other than the shorts, shirt, gaiters and boots I had worn in the desert, plus a Sten gun and clips of ammunition of which I was quickly divested. Like all good officers he handed me over to the Station Warrant Officer who lost no time in issuing me with an ill-fitting uniform from the stores, arranging a railway warrant to Poynton and making me sign for those and two pounds cash (I had no English money). He couldn't get the scruffy airman, me, off his Valley airfield soon enough. I didn't argue – I went.

Totally unexpected I arrived home at Poynton, suntanned, badly in need of a haircut but with my canister of grapes proudly tucked under my arm. A great luxury – they were the first grapes anyone in the village had seen for over three years.

CHAPTER 11

Back to School

At this time my son, Bryan, was almost four months old. During the time I had been away he had been very ill, but hospital treatment together with careful nursing by his mother had corrected the problem and he was now making good progress. Both the baby and Nora were living with her mother at the general provisions shop on London Road South. My mother-in-law was always pleased to see me and made me most welcome, even on this occasion when I had neither ration coupons nor money.

I had been home several days before the implications of this state of affairs dawned on me. Since I had been seconded to the Airborne Division the RAF had no means of knowing where I was. I might be still in North Africa, or Sicily. It was most unlikely they would ever think that I had managed to wangle myself back to England. After three weeks at home I came to the conclusion that, pleasant as my unofficial leave was, sooner or later the authorities would catch up with me. One morning I cycled to the RAF camp at Wilmslow and, after being passed from one section to another finished up in the Padre's office! After listening patiently to my story he gave me £2 out of the station welfare fund, told me to go back home and promised to contact me again in a few days time. This he did and once again I cycled over to Wilmslow, this time to receive orders to report to Hurn and a railway warrant to enable me to travel there.

Just outside Chichester the airfield at Hurn was crammed with aircraft and Horsa gliders. It seemed that I could not get away from the Airborne Division. Number 295 was the towing squadron, with not only the usual mix of Albermarles and Halifaxes, but also half a dozen Whitleys. In the autumn of 1943 these were a rare sight indeed, but I was pleased to see them, even more so when I was allocated to the Whitley flight for radio maintenance and testing. The old twin-engined bombers were not used as towing aircraft for the gliders but for paratroop training, for which they were ideally suited. Earlier in this narrative I mentioned that the first British paratroop operation of the war, Bruneval 1940, involved Whitleys.

It was when I was at Hurn that I witnessed one of the worst of the many tragedies of those days. One afternoon I was re-splicing a damaged aircraft aerial when I heard the familiar sound of a Whitley roaring down the runway on takeoff. Seconds later I looked up as a series of staccato explosions heralded trouble. Sure enough the port engine of the bomber was trailing smoke. Climbing to a height of about six hundred feet the left wing began to drop. I could visualise the pilot desperately trying to correct this, the only hope they had was to keep that wing high if they were to make any kind of controlled landing. It was not to be. The left wing went over even more, the bomber stalled, turned round 180 degrees and came screaming back down towards the airfield. Just before the perimeter fence the Whitley plunged into a cluster of trees. Immediately there was a column of dense oily black smoke and within seconds a pillar of flame. There was no way anyone could be got out of that inferno alive. As it happened no paratroopers were aboard, after a routine service the crew were air-testing the Whitley, so the casualty-list was not as bad as it could have been but, I must admit, the incident set my nerves jangling again.

I had now had been issued with new kit, and my uniforms actually fitted me – which was a relief. I also started to be paid again, although it was to be many more months before I drew the money owed to me from my time in North Africa. It was now Autumn 1943 and it seemed obvious that preparations were beginning for the invasion of northern

Back to School

Europe sometime in 1944. As in North Africa the Airborne Division at Hurn were joined by their American counterparts. It came as a surprise to me when one day I was called into the Orderly Room and informed I had been selected for a training course at the RAF College, Cranwell. "Training for what?" I asked. "Wireless Mechanic, it says here," answered the Duty Officer, "never heard of that before." Neither had I. Despite my protestations that my purpose of being in the Air Force was to operate their wireless sets, not build them, to Cranwell I duly went.

Cranwell is located on the A17 between Newark and Sleaford in Lincolnshire. A long-established permanent station it has fine buildings, barrack-blocks and, of course parade grounds. It is here that in peacetime would-be pilots receive their initial training and, if successful, become commissioned officers. That situation, I believe, still appertains today. Of course I was not one of those exalted beings. I was in a barrack block with fifty-or-so others, designated to be wireless mechanics. All were qualified wireless operators, but I was the only operator/air gunner amongst them. This gave me many hours of amusement, because of my additional trade and past experiences the rest of the class had the mistaken idea that I knew what the future held for us. The more I protested that I had no, idea, the less they believed me.

The course itself was not too difficult, being mainly concerned with emergency repairs if for any reason the equipment failed. The training was obviously meant for ground maintenance only, it would be impossible to manipulate a soldering iron flying in an aircraft during night time – or day time!

Despite the war Cranwell maintained many of its peacetime habits. Once a month our class was detailed for the Sunday morning Church Parade. Then with the RAF band heading the long column of religious captives with a stirring march we would strut through the camp to hear the Padre explain that as God was on our side there was no way we could lose the war. A few hundred miles away we had no doubt that some German preacher was telling our enemies exactly the same thing. On the other three no-Church Parade weekends it was every man for himself. On the Saturday afternoon I would walk out of the main gate and tramp the ten miles to Newark. There I would get on a train to Sheffield – without a ticket, naturally – and board a Manchester-bound train where, thanks to my previous railway experience I had no difficulty in crossing platforms to finish my journey home to Poynton. It was always very late at night when I did arrive home, often I had to throw pebbles at Nora's bedroom window to waken her so that she would come down and let me in the house. I don't think I ever disturbed son Bryan in his slumbers, but within minutes of me creeping up the back stairs of number 41, there would be a knock on the connecting door to number 39 and Nora's mother would appear with a mug of tea and a sandwich.

Returning to Cranwell on the following day, Sunday, was different. Both my wife and mother-in-law were insistent that I obeyed the rules, at least as far as paying my fare was concerned. So my route back was a little different. A bus to Manchester, then from the Central station (now defunct) to Doncaster where I changed for Newark. Once there I had the ten mile tramp to Cranwell. My arrival time at Newark was about two o'clock in the morning. There was a total wartime blackout, although I doubt there are many street lamps between Newark and Cranwell even today. In those days, being young and fit, the long walk in the dark never bothered me – except on one occasion. This was one particularly silent and black night. There was no moon nor the sound of any aircraft, either friendly or hostile. I had just passed the Stragglethorpe crossroads, about two miles outside the village of Leadenham, when I sensed – rather than heard – someone, or *something*, following me. I halted, and sure enough there were two footsteps behind me before they also ceased. Strange footsteps too, they gave a sort of pit-a-pat sound. I started walking again, and once more suddenly came to a halt. Sure enough the pit-a-pat noise was there again, just one

Back to School

footstep this time. Once again I strode forward, then summoning up all my courage quickly turned and lunged at the shadowy figure behind me. There was a startled squeak as I grabbed him by the throat. It was another Cranwell trainee, also tramping from Newark back to the camp. He had been nervous of the eerie footsteps in front of him, which was me, and his feet were hurting so badly that he had taken off his boots and was walking in his stocking feet. That explained the pit-a-pat footsteps behind me. By the time we avoided the military police, crawling under the perimeter wire to gain access we were the best of friends. I never knew his name, nor would I have recognised him in the light of day.

One Monday morning together with several hundred other airmen I was on parade in the main square for the ceremonial hoisting of the RAF flag. Having only crawled into my bed three hours before after another illicit visit home I was feeling extremely tired and hoping for a short lie-down in the barrack room before reporting to my class. I was far from pleased, therefore, when the Warrant Officer conducting the ceremony instead of dismissing us yelled for the parade to "stand fast" while a special announcement was made. Up on to the dais stepped an elderly Flight Lieutenant. Nervously clearing his throat he squeaked "Is there a Goodwin on parade?" Before I could decide how to get away a dozen of my "friends" who they vowed later only did it because they thought I was going to be presented with a medal, assured him there was and helpfully pointed to me.

"Ah," said the officer, "I have an urgent message for you. Your wife and child are both well and she promises to write to you soon."

That was the answer to my radio communication from Tunisia and proved the efficiency of the RAF in looking after the welfare of its personnel. However, seeing that I had only left my wife a few short hours before the trouble they had taken really was a waste of time. Still, I suppose it is the thought that counts.

Some Were Lucky

CHAPTER 12

Mobile Menaces

The Cranwell training course finished in February 1944 and I then found myself a triple tradesman – Wireless Operator/Mechanic – Air Gunner, or WOM/AG for short. I do not believe there were many of us around. Once again I found myself down on the South coast, this time at Thorney Island from where daylight sweeps over northern France by light bombers and fighter-bombers were almost a daily event. I only saw one heavy bomber land there. That was a Halifax which one morning came screaming out of the clouds, minus the whole of its tail section, the figures of two of its crew following close behind having managed to claw their way out of the crashing aircraft, but at a height far too low for their parachutes to be effective. They were unlucky. The bomber made a huge crater in the middle of the airfield and there was little left for anyone to clear away. The dead rear gunner was found in his detached turret some three miles further up the coast. Halifaxes were made in bits and pieces in countless small manufacturing units countrywide and assembled at the Handley Page main factory. A story prevalent at the time was that there had been several cases of the rear section of the fuselage coming "unstuck" with the obvious disastrous results.

My stay at Thorney was to be but a short one, after only two weeks came orders to report to an RAF unit at Pwllheli in North Wales. This was an area with which I was quite familiar due to having toured the district on cycling holidays prior to the war. I was quite curious as to what I was going to join there, there was no airfield of any consequence located near that I knew of, certainly none large enough to cope with any operational unit I had previously been involved with. As always, I had to wait until I arrived before I could find out.

One of the bitter lessons of 1940 had been the loss of so much of the British forces equipment simply because so very few servicemen were able to drive. If there were no qualified driver, for whatever reason, that inevitably meant that particular unit's vehicle had to be abandoned. The authorities were determined that this should not happen again, and in preparation for the coming invasion as many personnel as possible, Army, Navy and Air Force, should be taught to drive.

Pwllheli was one of the places chosen as an instructional centre. What had been pre-war boarding houses were converted into billets for the trainees, and the triangle formed by the Lleyn Peninsula – Caernarvon – Criccieth was ideal for teaching novice drivers and endangering the least possible number of other human beings. Unfortunately not a great deal of consideration was given to the local sheep.

Two weeks was the allotted time in which to reach the necessary standard to pass a driving test and acquire a service driving licence. A wide variety of vehicles were provided for practise, ranging from the Ford V8 (a large, powerful, American saloon which none of us had ever seen before except in Hollywood gangster films), Jeeps, lorries and last but far from least the "Queen Mary's" – a long articulated lorry. Part of the driving test was reversing one of the latter up to a lamp standard and just touching it. Knock it over and the result was failure. No one ever got a second chance but, surprisingly enough, whilst I was there no lamp standards were uprooted although most were either bent or leaning at crazy angles.

There was a ratio of only one instructor to every three learners. After the introductory talk and lesson all four would climb into a Ford V8 and the pupils would take turns to drive. Synchromesh was non-existent on all vehicles and gear-changing was a matter of correct engine revolutions and double-declutching. The noisy grating of gears around the hitherto peaceful Snowdonia was horrendous.

After the first day the instructor would take one pupil on the four-hour morning session, and another one on a similar period in the afternoon. The other two learners went solo on any vehicle allocated to them, a car, van or heavy lorry. "Queen Mary's" were never on the road without a qualified driver in the cab as well. As there was little other traffic about on the roads of that part of Wales the only real danger to life and limb was to the enthusiastic men in the driving seat of the military vehicles. Needless to say, within a day or two of starting the course various tea shops had been found, with discreet parking facilities, where unsupervised learners could spend a pleasant hour or so drinking tea, eating home-made scones, and play pontoon – or for the few hardened gamblers who had money to burn – a game of brag.

As always, on arrival at a new base one of the first priorities was to establish the virtues, or otherwise, of the female population. In Pwllheli there did not appear to be one. In their wisdom the RAF had not appointed any ladies of the service (the WAAF) to assist in the running of the unit. The possibilities of their temptation into a fate worse than death by randy airmen driving around the countryside in seemingly sumptuous luxury were all too obvious. The local inhabitants had also taken their own precautions. Dour Welshmen were plentiful, especially in the local hostelry, Sundays excepted. But their wives and daughters were kept, if not under lock and key, out of sight. As one of the fathers explained to me one night, it simply was not safe to let them out. If they were not knocked down, on what he called the Monte Carlo circuit of the town's main street, then some devious sex-mad airman would take advantage of their innocent trusting nature. Not an Englishman, they were gentlemen, he assured me gratefully accepting another pint, but certainly an Irishman or, worse still, a Scot. In his opinion they were the worst of all. Jamie Stewart, who came from Glasgow and sat at the bar with us, took this as a great compliment to the manhood of his nation.

"Seek and ye shall find" is an old adage. My fellow airmen at Pwllheli were seekers of the highest calibre and success soon came their way, they discovered that helping at some of the local farms were girls of the Land Army. These were young ladies who had voluntarily joined an organisation designed to assist farmers who had lost their normal male labour to the Forces, and a good job they did too. Their motto was "Back to the Land" which was naturally converted by servicemen to "backs to the land," with a different meaning altogether. Contact was craftily established by Jamie Stewart blocking a farm gate with his ten ton truck for twenty minutes while trying to do a three-point turn in an impossibly narrow lane. Meanwhile, an irate brunette, some twenty years of age, waited impatiently to open the gate and bring out the cows down to the farm buildings for milking.

It could hardly be classified as blackmail but by the time Jamie had admitted defeat in his attempts at a three-point turn it had been agreed that the following afternoon the girl would bring along three of her friends and would be delighted to go on a quick tour of the countryside. Jamie would arrange this.

In Jamie's own words, he, I and two others, each in their allocated vehicle for the day, whatever it might be, would meet these girls at the designated spot, and take them to a secluded place he had found, a mere six miles away, where we would have a picnic – plus anything else that might be on offer. The girls would supply the food, we the drink. Ivy, he said, was quite attractive but, having made the contact she was definitely his. The rest of us would have to take our chance. At this stage he hesitated a little before warning us of possible problems. To the untrained eye the girls of the Land Army may not appear to be all that attractive. Their thick green sweaters and jodhpur-style corduroy trousers not doing a great deal for their femininity. An odour of cow manure and other natural odours of the farmyard which clung to them could arouse sexual desire even more than an expensive perfume – once one got used to it.

With these words of encouragement ringing in our ears we turned up in convoy to meet the young ladies. Two of us were lucky, and I was one of them, having been allocated four-ton Bedford trucks, easy to drive and with comfortable seats. Poor Jamie had a battered open-top Ford car, on which the hood refused to operate, and a light drizzle compounded his misery. Much to his disgust the remaining member of our little band had a V8 saloon.

However, in general we had an enjoyable afternoon, marred slightly towards the end by the fact that Jamie's "secluded place" happened to be at the end of a cul-de-sac lane which, to avoid reversing nearly a mile back to the main road necessitated a three-point turn. The two cars managed it without too much difficulty but, although all four of us tried, we could not succeed in manoeuvring the Bedfords and had to slowly and painfully reverse out. This took quite some time and it was obvious we were going to be much later returning than we had intended. Unfortunately on arrival the cars had gone up the lane before the lorries, and there was no way they could squeeze past us to get out until we were clear ourselves. To say the girls were distraught would have been one of the understatements of the war, "Milking," they cried, "we are late for milking."

Jamie's reply to this is unprintable.

Suffice it to say that we never saw the young ladies again – more's the pity.

It was a wonderful two weeks for those fortunate enough to be on the driving course in North Wales. In the spell I was there the weather was mainly fine and mild and the beauty of the scenery, I found, could be much more readily appreciated from the seat of a powerful automotive than bending low over the handlebars as you wearily propelled a bicycle up one of the many hills.

At the end of the course I was successful in the driving test, to the best of my knowledge so was everyone else. Someone wasn't taking any risk of having to postpone the invasion because there were not sufficient qualified drivers on the books, and I suspect, the sooner we were out of North Wales the better for everyone concerned.

I awaited the next move the RAF had planned for me with interest. A Wireless Operator/Radio Mechanic/Air Gunner with a licence to drive anything up to a heavy tank. I could not imagine what the powers-that-be intended. An Airborne Division again, this time in some glider I had never heard of capable of transporting heavy lorries, or even "Queen Mary's," or perhaps a Ford V8 for a General? The day that the list of our various assignments were typed and pinned up on the notice board I joined the mob anxiously looking for their names and destinies. About halfway down mine appeared, Calshot.

Calshot?

Never heard cf it.

My rail warrant gave me the first clue. Southampton. After the usual tortuous journey of those days I eventually arrived at the southern port. On a wet and dismal evening the badly bomb-damaged area around the station did little to cheer me, nor did the Service Police on duty appear to take a great deal of interest in my requests for assistance in getting to my final destination. However, someone must have made a telephone call for after about three hours a car arrived from Calshot to take me to the base.

CHAPTER 13

Air Sea Rescue

The following morning I wearily struggled out of my two issued blankets to find that the hut in which I had been sleeping was at the end of a small peninsula jutting out into Southampton Water. There were some seaplanes moored offshore, not the Sunderlands I had known at Mountbatten, but the smaller Catalinas.

After breakfast I reported to the Orderly Room, unable to think in what way the training I had been given over the past months related to flying boats. Much to my surprise the corporal in charge appeared to be pleased to see me.

"Hope you didn't unpack all your gear last night," he said, "you're the first one to arrive for 2691 and we've had to put one of our own lads on guard aboard her. Get down to the jetty as quick as you can and go out and relieve him."

Luckily I hadn't done any unpacking at all so I was able to lug all my gear down to the small wooden pier where, tied up, was a small motor-dinghy containing a rather bored-looking scruffy airman.

"Excuse me," I said, "can you take me out to 2691?"

"Come to relieve old Bert, have you?" came the reply "he's been stuck out there for three days. Probably starved to death by now. Anyhow, hop aboard and we'll go and find out."

As requested I "hopped aboard" the dinghy which spluttered out into Southampton Water. To my surprise we went past the moored inshore Catalinas towards an anchored High Speed Launch. Her superstructure was painted battleship-grey and on the bows of her jet black hull were the numbers 2691. As we approached I looked at her in disbelief, a trained wireless operator, gunner, even radio mechanic.......maybe. But why the driving lessons?

"Bert" appeared as we came alongside, looking as if he had been on the launch for three weeks rather than three days, obviously having neither washed nor shaved whilst he had been on board, and possibly for quite some time before that. He couldn't scramble into the dinghy and change places with me fast enough. I stood disconsolately with my kitbag on the deck of the launch as she rocked slightly to the wash of the dinghy as it turned away back to the jetty. The last words I heard from Bert was something about the bread going stale and that he'd eaten the last of the sausages.

It was a Wednesday and it would be two days before the other members of the crew arrived. Bert had been right about the bread, and there was nothing else to eat, although there was tea, condensed milk and the fresh water tank was almost full. My fear of starvation was allayed when a supply boat came out to me on the first afternoon and stocked the launch with sufficient food to feed a complete crew for at least a fortnight.

Number 2691 was an Air Sea rescue launch. Displacing 25 tons she was sixty-eight feet long, powered with two Napier Sea Lion water-cooled engines she was capable of a speed of forty-two knots. Known as the Hants and Dorset class she was built by Thorneycroft and had an all-wooden hull. Her only protection was some armour plating in the wheelhouse. Above the wheelhouse was an open bridge, with loud hailer, searchlight and repeater compass. She was armed with two twin-Browning machine gun turrets, similar to those on Blenheim aircraft, situated amidships port and starboard and right aft on the stern a much more lethal weapon, a 20 mm Oerlikon cannon. Just behind the wheelhouse was the radio room, equipped with the latest Marconi transmitter and receiver, the T1154 and R1155, with which I had been used to operating in my flying days with 51 squadron. There was no radar. Below deck the crew's quarters extended about fifteen feet aft from the bow and then there was a narrow passage which connected past the skipper's cabin, a tiny compartment approximately six feet by eight feet, into the sickbay – where any rescued personnel could receive attention. A companionway, a flight of eight, 4 feet wide, steps then led up to the stern deck. The remainder of the launch below deck, almost forty feet, was taken up by the engine room with its Napier Sea Lion engines, an auxiliary diesel, dynamos, and – of course petrol tanks. In short, the boat was a volatile floating bomb.

On the Friday morning I had just finished clearing my breakfast dishes (one chipped plate and a tin mug) in the tiny galley-cum-kitchen when a heavy thump alongside heralded the arrival of the other members of the crew. There were now twelve of us altogether, including the skipper. A Flight Lieutenant named Field in civilian life he had been a greengrocer, so inevitably carried the nickname "Plum." The coxswain was a Flight Sergeant, "Chiefy," an ex-trawlerman and therefore the most experienced man aboard. The two engineers were both Geordies from North East England and the second wireless operator, "Pinto" Payne, was an eighteen-year old from Portsmouth. There were five deck hands, all trained gunners, and a medical orderly, obviously known as "Doc," completed our number.

It was now getting towards the end of May 1944 and as far as the eye could see Southampton Water was crowded with all sorts of craft, from the familiar outlines of Royal Navy destroyers, frigates and cruisers to strange floating structures the like of which none of us had ever seen before. We were to find out later that these were sections of the floating Mulberry harbour which was to play such a vital role off the Normandy beachhead. Not that we had that much time to look around us. Making sure that our own craft became fully operational meant working day and night for the next few days. Stowing away the gear and personal belongings of the crew was a job in itself in the limited space available. There were only four bunks for weary bodies to rest upon, the other seven slept anywhere suitable they could find. Maybe the skipper was the most uncomfortable of all curled up in his tiny cabin on a bunk which was barely five feet long. The engines were turned over briefly when we moved the launch to the base to top up the fuel tanks, the real test of their efficiency would be when we received our sailing orders. These came the following day, we were to move to Weymouth.

It was an easy passage. The sea was calm and visibility good. The launch moved along at a steady ten knots until the Needles were astern, then speed was gradually increased until the bows lifted clear of the sea and a huge white wake streamed behind us. In no time at all we had passed Bournemouth and Swanage to starboard and were entering Weymouth Bay. At anchor here were a great many ships ranging from peacetime passenger liners to naval landing craft for either tanks or infantry. A tempting target for enemy aircraft, but such was the Allied air supremacy at the time that only during darkness did the odd hit-and-run low flying raider cause trouble. The main danger to life and limb was not from the intruder but the light and medium anti-aircraft barrage fired frantically over Weymouth by the ships out in the bay.

We were instructed to berth at the town quay, which is from where in happier times the ferry services sail to Cherbourg and the Channel Islands. When we arrived there it was to discover that we had two other boats for company. One was an Air Sea rescue high speed launch, identical to ourselves, but bearing the number 2707, and the other an old paddle steamer which, before she was conscripted into the Royal Navy, had transported happy holiday-makers between Portsmouth and Ryde on the Isle of Wight. Over the next few weeks we were to become very good friends.

The area around the inner port of Weymouth showed the wear and tear of almost five years of war. There was hardly a building in sight without shattered windows and missing roof tiles, havoc wreaked by cannon and machine gun fire from

Air Sea Rescue

Crews of HSLs 2691 and 2707 Weymouth 1944

German fighters and bombers, and more recently added to by the trigger-happy sailors out in the bay. What had once been a dockside office of some sort or other had now been adapted by the RAF as the operational headquarters for launches 2691 and 2707. Whilst the location could not have been more convenient, the two boats being berthed only the width of the road away, we were worried because operational orders were given to us over, as far as we knew, an unsecured telephone line. Maybe we were concerned unnecessarily, from June the first no private telephone calls were allowed out of Weymouth, and postal services were suspended. All leave was cancelled and the whole of southern England became a no-go area. The folks at home must have wondered what had happened to their loved-ones when no letters arrived from them and it was impossible to contact them by 'phone.

Some Were Lucky

CHAPTER 14

D-Day the Invasion

On the afternoon of June the fourth the 'phone in our quayside office rang, and we were briefed for our role in the invasion of Normandy. Although no experts we had our doubts. There was a steady downpour of rain and the wind gusted around the quayside and buildings. Sure enough, about seven o'clock in the evening came the postponement signal, although we were instructed to stay on immediate standby. Twenty-four hours later the weather had improved slightly and, together with hundreds of thousands of others, we were given the order to go.

We left Weymouth at 3.30 in the morning of the sixth of June. There was a stiff south-westerly breeze blowing, and as we left the shelter of Portland Bill HSL2691, working up to about thirty knots to overtake the slower invasion craft which had left some hours before, bounced from the crest of one ten foot high wave to the next. The historic grandeur of the occasion was somewhat lost upon us as we struggled to keep the contents of early morning breakfast in our stomachs. Most of us just managed do to that, until we arrived at our "rendezvous" position. This was about ten miles to the north of the port of Cherbourg (then held by the Germans) and to the west of where the Americans were landing on the Normandy beaches known by the code names "Omaha" and "Utah." Calculating that we were in the correct position the skipper gave the order to cut the engines, the launch lost way and, turning beam on to the sea, began a sickening, dizzy roll..........and how she rolled! To starboard 45 degrees, then over to port 45 degrees. Below deck there was the sound of crashing gear, pots, pans, crockery and everything else that wasn't securely fastened down. Only the skipper and our trawlerman coxswain cared if we lived or died, the rest of us were too busy being ill.

This state of affairs went on for over three hours. A few miles to the east of us fighting raged on the beaches. Battleships, cruisers and destroyers bombarded inland targets, landing craft scurried to and fro landing reinforcements and bringing off the wounded. Where we were the din of war was only faintly to be heard over the howling of the wind and the groans of the seasick.

Because of aircrew training my action station was on the bridge, from where I was able to operate the radio-telephone, Aldis lamp (for visual signalling), be responsible for aircraft identification and, perhaps most importantly, gunnery control of the two Bristol-type gun turrets, with their four Browning machine guns, and the Oerlikon cannon on the stern. I huddled in the starboard corner of the bridge, the central position was taken by the skipper, and George Legge (a Channel Islander) was the port-side lookout.

Having parted with my breakfast and feeling slightly better, although I had doubts about the future of my tea of the previous day, I suddenly became aware of several dots in the sky which were rapidly coming towards us. I gave a preliminary warning over the intercom system.

"Aircraft approaching from astern. Stand by."

The Oerlikon gunner, Jimmy, was a boy only eighteen years old. I looked back as he took the tremendous risk of negotiating the heaving deck to get to the stern. By some miracle he got there, and managed to fasten the safety strap which secured him to the gun and made sure that he would not be swept overboard as the weapon rotated through 360 degrees.

The incoming aircraft were now much closer. When they were about two miles away, and flying at a height of a thousand feet, they altered course slightly to our starboard side. This gave me a clear view and recognition was easy. In their earphones the gunners heard the voice of their controller:

"Hold your fire, check, check, check," I said, "aircraft are friendly."

They were Beaufighters, but not all that friendly.

To my horror they suddenly changed formation and went in line astern. I knew what that meant.

The leader tipped one wing and started to scream down towards us. I grabbed the Very light pistol and fired a flare giving the identification colour of the day. The response from the Beaufighter was a burst of cannon fire churning up the sea around us. His number two, following closely behind him began with machine guns and added to the fun by firing two rockets.

Swift as rockets are it is doubtful if the two fired by the Beaufighter moved any faster than, the crew of 2691. George Legge, hotly pursued by the skipper, disappeared from the bridge leaving me a poor third in the race to get to the illusory safety of the radio room. By the time I arrived there the operator, "Pinto" Payne could not be seen for the heaving mass of humanity crammed into the place.

I don't believe my feet touched one step of the companionway, certainly the coxswain's didn't as he landed on top of me in the sickbay. The rear end of "Doc," the medical orderly, protruded from under the bunk in the skipper's cabin, otherwise we appeared to have this particular part of the boat to ourselves. For some seconds there seemed to be a lull in the proceedings. Suddenly realising my responsibilities I warily crawled back up the steps of the companionway and poked my head out of the door. As I did so, a few feet away from me the engine room hatch was flung open and the heads of the two engineers popped up. In ripe Geordie language they both demanded to know what was going on.

Before I could reply a third Beaufighter came roaring in at sea level with cannons blazing. I had a brief impression of one of the engine room ventilators being blown over the side as simultaneously both heads of our valiant engineers disappeared and the hatch slammed shut again. Their question had been answered and curiosity satisfied.

I stayed where I was, at the top of the companionway, lying on my stomach with my head and shoulders out on the open deck. Common sense prevailing (or was it fatalism?) I realised there was little point in doing anything else. Certainly on such a small target there was nowhere to hide. Then, slowly, I became aware of two things. My seasickness had gone, and for some minutes everything had been quiet. Warily I got to my feet and looked around. The sky was empty. The Beaufighters had disappeared. Later, we learned that the last attacker had spotted the white star painted on our forecastle deck and correctly identified us as friendly.

Friendly! Our sole purpose in being there was to save airmen if they came down in the sea!!

When eventually we sorted ourselves out we were amazed to find that none of the crew had been hurt, nor had 2691 suffered any major damage. In addition to the ventilator the searchlight had been blown overboard and the loud-hailer had two neat bullet holes through it. Several other holes of various dimensions, from either cannon shells or machine gun fire were visible in the superstructure but there appeared to be nothing seriously wrong and the engines started without any trouble.

Wisely the skipper decided to call it a day and we set course for Weymouth where, on arrival, we were greeted as the heroes that we certainly were not. This was because of all the craft involved in the Normandy invasion which had sailed from the Dorset port we were the first to return, and so attracted a lot of attention.

It had been quite a day and we were all very weary. Our Navy friends on the paddle steamer berthed next to us on the quay brought welcome hot food and tea liberally laced with rum. They examined our battle scars with awe and we began to feel quite proud of ourselves. The fact that they had been inflicted by our own side didn't seem to matter quite so much.

CHAPTER 15

Win Some – Lose Some

A rest of two days was considered ample by the powers-that-be for us to fill in the holes in 2691 and replace, courtesy of Portland naval base, any missing parts. We never did manage to obtain a new loud-hailer, but the one we had worked, and the two bullet holes always impressed visitors, especially reporters from the press and radio. Our friendly paddle-steamer, used as a communications link with ships in the Bay, somehow wangled us on to the official rum issue list of the Royal Navy. Such is the wonderful efficiency of the records of our armed forces that, having once got on to the spirit list we stayed there, even later when we had moved to another base.

Our living conditions were also greatly improved by providing shore sleeping accommodation for the crew. Together with "Pinto" Payne I shared one bedroom in a requisitioned semi-detached house about ten minutes walk from the quay. The only furniture in the room was two air force beds, with the usual three "biscuits" (very firm foam-filled cushions) serving as mattresses while two blankets each completed our luxurious quarters. There were no facilities for washing either clothes or ourselves but, as we discovered the first time we slept there either the bedding we had been given was not very clean, or perhaps it was a legacy from the previous occupants, but we had with us some very hungry fleas.

Flight Lieutenant Field, our skipper, had also made arrangements to sleep ashore. He found himself extremely nice quarters with all home comforts. Rumour had it that the lady with whom he was billeted was a lonely widow anxious to do her best for the war effort.

June ninth found us back at work again. We now began a system of one day at sea, whilst our fellow launch, 2707, would stay as a reserve in harbour and the following day the boats would change duties. This did give us the chance of some rest, even if every other night we had to sleep as best as we could on board. However, it made a change from the fleas.

There was still a fairly stiff breeze resulting in a heavy swell in the Channel, making life as difficult as ever when we reached our rendezvous positions and rolled beam-on to the waves. It was impossible to cook any food in the galley so packets of sandwiches (always corned beef) were made up and given to us before we sailed. After the second time this had happened none of us, with the exception of "Pinto" could eat them. I can remember no more revolting sight during the war than my fellow wireless operator coming up to the bridge with a thick corned beef sandwich, taking a huge bite at it, chewing frantically, swallowing, and seconds later leaning over the side and vomiting. He then repeated the procedure until the sandwich had been totally consumed – and rejected. His earnest belief was that it was not good to be seasick on an empty stomach. The rest of us would have nothing to eat or drink after breakfast in harbour, usually about 4 am, until we returned at nightfall. A few tots of the navy rum helped to keep us going while we were at sea.

It was on our third trip out that we had our first success. On this occasion we had been ordered to a position much further to the west than ever before so that the Channel Islands lay almost due south of us and although we were well out to sea a keen watch was kept for enemy aircraft and E-boats which, if they ventured out from Cherbourg would mean trouble in a big way. They were not only faster than the RAF launches but were also much more heavily armed.

We had been lying with engines stopped for almost two hours, as always beam-on to the never-ending heavy swell. The monotonous rolling from port to starboard and, after a sickening pause back again, had a hypnotic effect. Wedged in my corner of the bridge I was finding concentration becoming difficult. As the boat rolled, I found myself first looking up at the clouds scudding across the sky, and a minute or so later, down into green water. Apart from the shrieking of the wind through the radio aerials there was not a sound. For once even the chattering of Morse in my earphones had ceased and we were too far away from the Normandy beachhead to hear gunfire.

Suddenly there was the boom of an explosion.

Right in front of me was the alarm button which activated bells in the wheelhouse, radio and engine rooms and all other compartments. There was no need to press it on this occasion as the crew scrambled from below deck to their action stations and the engines started up with a roar. From his cabin "Plum" Field arrived on the bridge.

"What the hell's going on," he demanded, "and why the devil are we going round in circles?"

"If someone will tell me," came the calm voice of "Chiefy" from the wheelhouse, "I'll know what course to steer."

It was George Legge who spotted the smudge of smoke in the sky, some five miles away, and it was our redoubtable skipper, with the aid of powerful binoculars (provided we believed by the Weymouth widow) who excitedly reported four parachutes descending.

"Let the dog see the rabbit," came the comment of "Chiefy," and 2691 steadied on a course towards them.

We were there in a matter of minutes, and came down to a slow speed to search the area. Out of the four we found only one, the cold sea had quickly taken the others. The sole survivor, out of the crew of eleven, was the navigator of an American Liberator (B27 I think they called them). Suffering from shock and hypothermia, after treatment by "Doc" he was able to tell us that the Liberator had caught fire for no apparent reason and he had just had time to bale out before the aircraft exploded.

At full speed we returned to Dorset and Portland where, as requested by radio, an ambulance awaited our survivor. As we off-loaded him we basked in the admiration of a number of watching Royal Navy Wrens. Apparently RAF HSL2691 was acquiring quite a reputation. We were soon to become even more famous – and wish we hadn't.

Refuelling at Portland we set off to return to our designated position, but were barely clear of Portland Bill when, a hundred yards or so on our starboard side we saw what appeared to be the wake of a periscope. To the jangle of alarm bells the gunners rushed to their stations and, encouraged by the greengrocery language of the skipper over the loud-hailer, young Jimmy on the Oerlikon blasted away 20mm shells at the target.

"It's a Jerry midget submarine, we need help. Get some quick!" yelled "Plum."

It was at that very moment that the leader of a destroyer flotilla began to emerge from Portland harbour. Calling its attention to us with the Aldis lamp I passed the message that we had located and were engaging an enemy submarine. Acknowledging the signal the destroyer rapidly picked up speed, smoke streaming from her funnels and an enormous white bow wave indicating her enthusiasm to join in the action. Just as impressive were the other five destroyers who shot out of the harbour after her, equally determined to play their part.

Meanwhile HSL2691 was careering round in ever decreasing circles, all guns blazing, but having no apparent effect on the target.

"Stand by to ram!" screamed our intrepid skipper.

The language of "Chiefy," our coxswain, when he heard this can only be found in the dictionary especially compiled for Grimsby trawlermen. Translated into everyday English he politely drew the attention of his commanding officer that the craft on which we served his Majesty King George was constructed of wood. Ramming the steel plates of a submarine would certainly sink the attacker and not even scratch the attacked.

This short, but explicit, discourse was ended when the leading destroyer peremptorily ordered us out of the way. We did, and waited breathlessly for the depth charges to blow our enemy out of the water. Nothing happened. The destroyer passed by the spot and then, to our astonishment circled round and came to a stop. After several minutes she got under way again and sent this signal :

"Congratulations. You have been fighting a paravane and actually hit it. There is one hole, otherwise completely serviceable."

A paravane is a contrivance used by minesweepers for cutting the moorings of submerged mines. The one with which we had been fighting a battle had been lost by a sweeper a week previously, and its apparent movement through the water was simply an effect created by the tide.

That incident might have been forgiven, had we not a few days later been the originators of a radio message which brought out the same destroyers to chase enemy E-boats which weren't there. Once again we had been thirsting for action and, in asking for instructions, somehow we had mixed up the code.

Then there was the coming into harbour incident. The skipper had blessed us with the idea that if we lined the deck in naval fashion upon entering and leaving harbour we might conceivably raise our sunken prestige. The deck-dressing drill was carried out perfectly three times, to the awe and admiration of the Yankees on board the LCI's (landing craft – infantry) in the harbour.

Whether or not the Royal Navy noticed we never knew, but of course they just had to be watching the day we cruised by our gallant American allies when they showered our deck with packets of cigarettes and the seven deck hands standing rigidly at attention, broke ranks in order to get their share.

After that unfortunate affair the skipper was a broken man, and even 2691 herself seemed to skulk in and out of the port. For days on end we had gone out to what had now become a routine rendezvous midway between Portland Bill and

Cherbourg, and all we had seen in that time was a corvette which had asked us to move as she wished to drop depth charges in our position. When we had hurriedly shifted she steamed past and threw her garbage over the side.

Then came the day when we had been out since just before dawn and the sun was beginning to set as we waited impatiently for the signal to return to base. The eight foot swell in which we had wallowed uncomfortably all day began to look increasingly formidable as the dwindling light transformed the sea from dull grey to menacing black.

From somewhere to the south-east came a dull explosion. A hurried consultation of the charts, however, revealed that another rescue launch should be in that vicinity and we were not justified in leaving our position to investigate unless we were called upon to do so by the naval authorities. Except for the usual routine calls the radio remained silent and, apart from the howl of the rising wind and the slap, slap of the water against our hull we were alone and, apparently, forgotten.

I had just decided that the noise we had heard had been the sound of an exploding mine, and hopefully a recall to Weymouth was imminent, when our call sign (MHB19) came spluttering through on the wireless. To my surprise it was not base but another rescue launch, our friend 2707. The operator seemed to be having difficulty in sending his message, for the Morse was slow and there were uneven pauses in his sending. The message, decoded, ran : "Unable make headway. Many wounded on board. Require assistance – urgent."

As the operational orders had placed 2707 in the locality in which we had heard the explosion we immediately leaped to the conclusion that it was she who had been attacked. Setting course towards her at the best speed we dared, in that sea even thirty knots made the ride very bumpy, we relayed her message to base with the information that we were going to her aid.

Ten minutes after we had started off towards her another signal, this time with SOS priority, came over the air.

"Have 120 survivors H.M.S. Blackwood aboard, many seriously injured. Sea worsening, heavy roll, please hurry."

A twenty-five ton launch, overall length 68 feet, is not meant to carry over 130 men, for together with her crew of twelve that is what our friends had on board. In the sea then running we were afraid she would capsize before we could reach her. Our only hope was in finding her quickly, and in the stygian blackness there was only one way. We asked her to send out continuous radio transmissions so that we could "home" on to her with our direction-finding apparatus.

This was liable to bring unwelcome visitors to the scene in the form of E-boats, but that was a chance which had to be taken. The spray sweeping over the bridge as we bucketed along made visibility almost nil and, to add to our troubles it started to rain. "Chiefy," the coxswain, in the wheelhouse had a continuous fight to keep the needles of the direction finder visual meter dead centre, but when they began to kick violently we knew that we were near.

Suddenly, a few hundred yards ahead, a red Very light soared into the air. We slowed engines and switched on our searchlight. The sight which met our eyes was unbelievable. Instead of the launch we were expecting to see there was a mass of humanity alternately appearing and then disappearing in the troughs of the waves. Crowded on the deck of 2707, back to back, clinging to her guns, Carley floats, superstructure and mast were sailors, many wearing nothing but trousers – and a few not even those. We closed until we were within about twenty feet. Switching on the loud-hailer the skipper called across the dividing angry space:

"How many do you want us to take off you?"

"Every man you can get aboard," boomed back from the other bridge, "I have some amputation cases here and nowhere they can be properly looked after."

"Plum" snapped out his orders. Down went the crash nets and fenders and the distance between the two boats gradually decreased. I don't know what the rest of the crew were thinking, but as I watched the other launch loom above us one minute whilst the next we were threatening to crash down on her deck I didn't feel very happy. Luckily – or to give both coxswains their due – skilfully, we hit each other at just the right moment. Even so there was a splintering of wood as their rubbing strip sheared almost the whole length of our beam.

Encouraged by both skippers, sailors began to jump from 2707 on to our boat, clutching tiny bundles of personal belongings which they had managed to save from their own doomed ship. Every able man was transferred to 2691 and "Doc," our nursing orderly, made the perilous trip in the reverse direction so that he could give assistance to the seriously injured on the journey home.

The launches managed to pull away from each other without causing any major damage, but as we ourselves now had 90 men aboard we had trouble of our own. The shivering survivors from the torpedoed, or mined, frigate – they were not sure which – were crammed into every conceivable nook and cranny. The forecastle held 30, the sickbay another 25, the skipper's cabin 6, the wheelhouse and companionway another dozen.

The engine room, and even the after locker, were utilised and when I had pushed 4 bedraggled matelots into the tiny wireless cabin with "Pinto" I knew why the operator of 2707 had found it difficult to transmit his Morse.

Eight knots was the best speed we could make, but the Navy, who by this time had realised the trouble we were in, had despatched two more rescue craft to our aid. Once again radio homing signals guided them to us, and once again the same breathtaking procedure was gone through until our load was evenly distributed and the launch became more stable.

Then came the snag; we had been wallowing about in the strong crosswind in mid-Channel so much that no one could be certain of our position. Above everything else our small convoy had to avoid making a landfall at the wrong place. The dangers to small craft on the blacked-out English south coast were many. Portland Race was only one of them.

"Plum" Field was in one of his (all too rare) inspired moods.

"Tell 'em all to follow us," he ordered me.

I wondered how the Navy boys would react to an RAF launch behaving as if it had another Nelson in command, but they acknowledged my signal and obediently fell in line astern as we confidently led the way through the now heavy seas.

Meanwhile, our passengers took things very calmly, although from time to time they expressed some concern as we rolled over to an almost vertical angle. They were nowhere near as worried as the watch on the bridge when our estimated time of arrival had been overrun by fifteen minutes without a sign of land. The other boats followed us faithfully, their dimmed navigation lights spasmodically showing as they plunged in our wake. The coxswain had just been given the order to alter course when, from dead ahead, came the challenging flicker of the Portland Bill lookout station.

From there on it was plain sailing. Waiting ambulances at Portland quickly took away our passengers and we were given a good Navy breakfast, and an extra ration of rum, before we returned to our berth for refuelling.

That we had led the other craft safely back to harbour, when they hadn't the vaguest idea where they were, delighted our crew more than the fact that we had pulled off our first real job without a hitch. It was hardly surprising that the following morning the crew of our paddle-steamer neighbour saw that HSL2691 had the name "Pathfinder" emblazoned on her bow. George Legge was quite an artist.

There was, however, something which not many people knew. In the excitement one of our deck hands had moved the steel safe containing the code books to a place of safety in the wheelhouse.

Our compass was five degrees out.

The beachhead in Normandy was now firmly established, with some Allied fighter aircraft operating from forward airstrips in France. The number of sorties, especially by bombers over our section of the Channel was growing noticeably less every day.

Some Were Lucky

We were sent out only twice more from Weymouth to rendezvous positions. I remember them both for different reasons. On the first occasion we ventured a little too near Alderney and were warned off by a shell from one of the big German guns there which splashed in the sea much too close for comfort. HSL2691 retired hastily at full speed. The next time out was a glorious summer day, not a cloud in the sky and the sea as calm as the proverbial millpond. Again we were allocated a position off the Channel Islands but, after our previous fright, this time we kept below the horizon and, hopefully, out of enemy radar range. The hours passed without incident and, to our surprise and joy, the recall to Weymouth came in the early afternoon. About half the distance back to base had been made when, without any warning, the sun was obscured by mist and within minutes visibility was nil. Speed was reduced to a crawl of five knots, but after the episode of safely guiding to harbour the HMS Blackwood survivor's flotilla we had every confidence in the skill of our skipper's navigational ability. This was rudely shattered when, based on an estimated time of arrival he instructed the coxswain to alter course and steer due north. It seemed a stroke of genius, for the coxswain had hardly done so when we ran into a clear patch of the fog. There, dead ahead of us, and less then half a mile away were cliffs.

"Man the guns," yelled our redoubtable skipper, "we'll run in and have a quick look."

Over our pints in the quayside pub that night we tried to work out, steering north in the English Channel, which country we could expect to find other than England.

CHAPTER 16

A Move and a Miss

July came, and with it orders for 2691 to move to a more active operational area. Our new base was to be Gorleston on Sea, close to Great Yarmouth, at the estuary of the River Yare.

This was quite a long trip for the launch, eastward along the south coast, past the Isle of Wight and Beachy Head with a stop at Dover for refuelling. It was a warm, sunny day and the Channel a flat calm. We were not at all happy, for as we approached Dover the French coast was clearly visible. Any shipping passing through the Straits was monitored by enemy radar, and on crystal clear days like this one would also be under the scrutiny of powerful binoculars and telescopes. In 1944 traffic in the area was minimal and confined to Naval minesweepers and destroyers. This left the huge German guns based in the Cap Gris Nez area short of targets, so that they vented their spite in spasmodically shelling the town of Dover itself. Understandably the thought crossed our minds that 2691 would make a pleasant change for them. One of those shells landing within a hundred yards of us, let alone a direct hit, would have been enough to sink us. However, we were totally ignored.

It is highly probable that HSL2691 still holds the record for the minimum time in which any comparative craft of that size has entered Dover harbour, refuelled, and departed. Not until the North Foreland came abeam was speed reduced back to a more sedate fifteen knots, and a course set to cross the wide Thames estuary towards Felixstowe.

The Luftwaffe had not paid any daylight visits to this area for quite some time, nevertheless the bridge watch kept a keen lookout. We were about fifteen miles north of Margate when an aircraft was spotted flying very low and approaching us from the east. I had no difficulty in identification, it was a B17, a Flying Fortress. The gunners relaxed and "Plum" Field waved enthusiastically as the bomber passed over us at an altitude of no more than a hundred feet. I had a dreadful premonition that something was wrong, a feeling which was all too soon justified as, two minutes later, the American bomber plunged into the sea.

Within seconds the throttles of 2691 were opened and the bows lifted as her speed rapidly increased to maximum. It was too late. Out of nowhere, it seemed, a Royal Navy ML (Motor Launch) appeared and came alongside the Fortress, which was still afloat, by the time we arrived the aircrew had all been safely transferred to the ML. The RN Lieutenant in charge of the ML suggested that we took the bomber in tow and try to salvage her but, before we could even work out a way to do this, with a gurgling and bursting of air bubbles the B17 dipped her nose and slid beneath the water.

The naval craft, with the rescued airmen on board flashed us a farewell signal on her Aldis lamp : "Nice to have met you. One you missed this time. Hard luck. Hope you don't have too much bother."

Acknowledging the message, I turned to the skipper, who looked at the signal pad with a puzzled expression on his face.

"What the devil do they mean," he asked, "why should we have any bother?"

I couldn't answer that, but when we arrived at Gorleston just over three hours later we soon found out. We had just tied up alongside the quay when I received a peremptory summons to report immediately to the Base Commanding Officer. A military policeman made sure that I did exactly that, not even allowing me time to change from my filthy, once white, sweater and oil-stained battledress into a decent uniform. A much-decorated Wing Commander, purple with rage, demanded to know firstly; why I had not replied to top priority signals, and secondly, why 2691 had not obeyed orders transmitted originally in code and finally, in desperation at our silence, in plain language. I was at a loss to give any explanation, the wireless had been tuned to the correct frequency, of that I was certain, and neither "Pinto" in the radio room, or myself on the bridge linked with a headset which allowed me to listen to all signals, had heard our call sign once, never mind repeatedly. Once the officer's tirade had quietened down somewhat, I explained this to him.

"Your call sign is Seagull one nine, isn't it?" he demanded.

The penny dropped. Operations had not been calling us in Morse on the wireless, but by radio telephony. (At that time in its infancy. The system had a maximum range, under good conditions of twenty miles. The frequency being determined by small crystals, which controlled very accurately the wavelength, and were issued to operational units, like ourselves by sector controls. The one we had in our RT set had been given to us by Portland.)

I explained this to the irate Wing Commander. He looked at me with disgust.

"Why," he demanded, "didn't you put in the crystals for this sector that were given to you at Dover?"

There was only one answer I could give.

"Sorry, sir, but I was not given any crystals at Dover."

For a full minute there was a stony silence, during which his piercing gaze never left me.

"Very well," he said, "someone on 2691 was given them. Get back to your boat."

I went.

The reason for the Wing Commander's wrath was the fierce rivalry between the RAF Air Sea Rescue Service and a section of the Royal Navy doing a similar job. Whilst co-ordination between the two was excellent there was always keen competition for one to make more successful pick-ups of survivors than the other. On this particular occasion, the "ditching" of the B17 in the Thames estuary, the RAF control had been warned by the US Army Air Force of the impending crash, and the Flying Fortress was actually being guided towards 2691 which was known to be in the area. Frantic radio-telephone calls to the launch, to be on the alert had gone unanswered. Naturally they had, our radio set, not having the correct crystals, was tuned to the wrong wavelength.

The Navy launch had been on a routine patrol in the estuary when the American bomber literally dropped in its lap. No wonder that the Wing Commander was annoyed!

Two things were never revealed. Why Operations had never tried to contact us by wireless, in Morse, and which member of the crew had been given the crystals for the RT set at Dover. Whoever it was had not passed them on to either "Pinto" or myself. The only one of us to have stepped ashore at the port had been "Plum" Field himself, and that was to post a letter, presumably a farewell to the Weymouth widow.

CHAPTER 17

New Base – New Skipper

Our living conditions at Gorleston were a great improvement on those at Weymouth. The Cliff Hotel, about five minutes walk from where we were tied up at the quay, was a luxurious change from the one bleak bedroom in the semi-detached house at the Dorset port. I had a room to myself and a bathroom next door. There was a good laundry service, and the food and recreational facilities were excellent. That was, of course, when we were stood down from operations, which was not as often as we would have liked.

Although sometimes called out to search for RAF bombers believed to have come down in the North Sea, in the main we were supporting the American Army Air Force on their daylight mass raids on Germany.

Based further up the Yare from Gorleston at Great Yarmouth was a flotilla of Royal Navy Motor Torpedo boats. They would sally out during the hours of darkness to search for, and attack, enemy shipping moving along the Dutch coast and the Frisian Islands. Sometimes they got into dogfights when they met German E-boats, but the worst damage we saw the MTB's suffer was when they ran into a similar flotilla from Grimsby, and they blazed away at each other for quite a while before recognising they were fighting friends. Tragically, there were casualties to crews of both the Grimsby and Yarmouth boats.

Located at Felixstowe were RN motor launches (ML's), together with which the RAF boats were to provide cover for

American bombers and fighters. We had not been at Gorleston a week when our Weymouth colleague 2707 arrived. It was just like old times when she tied up behind us, but we missed the company and support of the old paddle steamer.

The method of arranging the rendezvous positions for the launches reminded me of the allocation of the Bay of Biscay patrols during my flying days with 51 squadron. Usually there were four boats involved, two RN and two RAF. Spaced out at twenty mile intervals the nearest launch to enemy territory was not very far away from the Dutch island of Texel, then a German stronghold, a Luftwaffe fighter base and harbouring a crack flotilla of E-boats. This was not the favourite position to have, but we took it in turns, progressing in steps from the one nearest to the English coast the first trip, until three operations later we were at the number four rendezvous off Texel. Then, to our relief, we started all over again from number one.

Occasionally the routine varied and, in response to reports of cries for help from crashing aircraft, American and British, we would make frantic dashes, on one occasion almost to the mouth of the Elbe, on another within twenty miles of the coast of Denmark and, perhaps the most nerve-wracking one of all, almost to Norway. We never found any survivors.

The latitude and longitude of each rescue boat on station was given to the navigators of the American squadrons at their briefings prior to each raid. The idea, which worked very well, was that if an aircraft was disabled over enemy territory they should endeavour to maintain as much height as possible to enable them to cross the coastline. Having done this they then flew a course which would take them to the first inshore launch (for example, off Texel) then fly from that boat to the next one, and so on until, with luck, they reached England. Should they be forced down into the sea there was a reasonable chance of rescue. They had further assistance from a B17 which flew at a height of over 20,000 feet above Colchester and acted as a radio link. This Flying Fortress could talk to allied aircraft who were deep into Germany, give them courses to steer when they were in trouble, and try to direct fighters to their aid.

We could no longer wallow and drift around as we had done in the English Channel. For this system to work it was essential that the boats were exactly in the positions given to the aircrews. This was achieved in a very simple but effective way. The North Sea between England and Holland is nowhere very deep. Small buoys were given to each launch, with a length of rope – about a hundred feet long – at the end of which was a block of concrete. On arrival at its position the launch would stop engines, the crew lower the concrete weight over the side and pay out the rope. The buoy then floated on the surface and, when it had drifted a couple of hundred yards away the boat would re-start engines, move back up to the buoy, and the whole procedure repeated over and over again until the recall signal came. One thing I liked about the arrangement was that it gave some blessed relief from the discomfort of beam-on rolling. If the sea was calm enough we could even manage to make a cup of tea, or cocoa, while we were creeping back up to the buoy.

Aware of the menace of the British Light Coastal Forces, 2691 was included in this category, the Germans had introduced a new type of mine. Although not immune to the magnetic and horned varieties the speed of this type of craft, usually, had taken them past the lethal range of these varieties. With Teutonic cunning, the enemy had introduced the Teller mine. About the size of a lady's hatbox these floated on the surface of the sea. If a high speed launch hit one of these the Teller would be flung in the air by the bow wash and explode with devastating effect. There was a story of an RAF launch hitting one, the mine soared into the air but, instead of going off with a bang, landed on the forward deck of the launch. Wisely, the crew left it severely alone and returned to port, where it was very carefully removed by experts and the skipper of the boat concerned got a medal for his bravery (?).

On 2691 we never saw a Teller, but we did have one interesting experience with the older type. It was a calm and misty morning, for which we were thankful as we had the number four rendezvous nearest to Texel. With engines stopped the launch had just broached on to the sea as two of the deck hands began to lower the concrete weight over the side. To their amazement it went down about eight feet and stopped.

"What the hell are you playing at?" bellowed "Plum" from the bridge.

"Sir, it won't go down!" came back the reply.

The skipper peered down into the sea.

"No wonder," he shouted, "you've got the bloody thing on a mine. Move further aft and try again."

They did, all of six feet, and lowered the weight again. This time it sank to the bottom without a hitch.

"It was on one of those moored mines," our redoubtable captain commented, "might even be one of our own. Careless of them really, we might have been hurt."

We stayed with that buoy all day, moving up to it whenever we had drifted too far away and, every time we did so, expecting to be blown to pieces. The climax of nervous tension came when we were ordered to return to base, and the skipper insisted that we not only retrieved the buoy but pulled up the weight again.

This was to be the last time that "Plum" Field was to take us to sea. There were no farewells, he just disappeared and we never learned where he had gone, or what he was doing. Arriving at Gorleston that night we were given a two day stand down and when we returned to the launch it was to find we had a new Flight Lieutenant in charge of HSL2691.

He was a much younger man, named Lindley, who before the war had been an architect in Skegness, and a completely different character from our previous skipper.

CHAPTER 18

Giving – and Receiving

By the end of July 1944 mass raids by the US Army Air Force became an almost daily occurrence. The formations of hundreds of Flying Fortresses usually crossed the English coast well to the south of our base at Gorleston so we only saw them when we were well out to sea on our rendezvous position and they were returning home. Their Thunderbolt and Mustang escort fighters, however, used to come screaming overhead just after we had left the safety of harbour. The crew of HSL2691 placed bets on which we would hear first, the bell on the Smith's Knoll buoy – about four miles offshore – or the racket of the Thunderbolts and Mustangs as they flew eastwards towards Germany.

It was not all one way traffic.

At this stage of the war the Luftwaffe raids on Britain had been mainly reduced to fighter-bomber incursions on the coastal regions. Norfolk, being the closest area to the German airfields, had more than its share of these raids. So frequently did they occur that the familiar warble tone of the air raid siren, warning of incoming aircraft, was augmented by the "Cuckoo" system.

Incoming fighter-bombers, flying at low level, were only picked up by radar as they approached the coast a few miles away. The normal air raid sirens then were then activated over the whole area. Royal Observer Corps "spotters" posted at vantage points (church towers and factory roofs for example) gave a further warning of imminent danger if they judged the enemy to be coming directly over their locality.

This was done by pressing a switch on the siren at their position which then emitted a "cuckoo" sound. Whenever this happened everybody was supposed to take cover. If the intruder was judged to be about to unload his bombs, usually indicated by the engine noise rising as the aircraft began to dive, a further movement of the siren switch changed the "cuckoo" sound to "oocuck."

I vividly remember this happening when, one evening, I was in the Gorleston cinema. Half way through the main film the "cuckoo" siren could be heard over the sound track. No one in the audience moved. A few minutes later came the "oocuck" siren, and immediately there was a crashing of seats being turned up as their occupants dived for cover on the floor. Seconds after came the crashing of a nearby exploding stick of bombs. The film carried on, although the dialogue was somewhat difficult to follow as the audience struggled to re-seat themselves. Again, there was not only the din of seats (this time being turned back down) but the lurid complaints of some of their occupants who, in the darkness of the cinema were unable to find handbags, cigarettes, toffees, or whatever else they had on their knees prior to the scramble for the illusory safety of the auditorium floor.

In addition to the fighter-bombers there were also other menaces to this area of East Anglia. The German weapons known as the V1 and the V2. The first was the pilotless flying bomb, christened the doodle-bug by the incorrigible Londoners, and the V2 which was a huge rocket, packed with high explosives, against which there was no warning and no defence. Neither were very accurate and, from time to time, one or the other would come straying into the Great Yarmouth region. The local population were extremely impressed (wrongly) of Teutonic thoroughness when a V2 rocket was reported to have landed in the centre of the A47 road exactly halfway on the eight mile straight stretch between Great Yarmouth and Acle. Whether or not this was true I never discovered, but if so, far from being a very accurate delivery, the rocket was a long way from its intended target of central London.

As well as being depressing and frustrating, it was also fascinating when, at our rendezvous position, and the skies were clear, to see the vapour trails of V2 rockets launched from enemy held territory and watch their progress as they arched across the heavens and began the downward plunge to earth on England.

The V1 or doodle-bug, the flying bomb, gave the crew of HSL2691 an interesting experience but, for many hours, a great deal of personal worry to myself. We were sent out at dusk, a most unusual time and stranger still, to a position to the north of our base some fifteen miles out to sea from Skegness. It was a still, calm night, no moon and black as pitch. With engines stopped we had rocked gently around for two hours when a coded wireless message informed us to expect low flying friendly aircraft in the vicinity.

Some time later came an uneven drone of aircraft engines approaching from the east.

"Must be one of our night fighters," said the skipper to me, "what do you make of it?"

I was not only uncertain, but uneasy as well.

"Well it is not a Lancaster or Halifax, but neither does it sound like a Mosquito or Beaufighter. It's a two engined job, whatever it is, but they're not synchronised."

The vroom-vroom of the aircraft came ever closer. Lindley came to a quick decision.

"Switch on our navigation lights," he ordered, "it must be one of ours in trouble. Let him know we're here."

I yelled down to "Chiefy" in the wheelhouse and seconds later our port and starboard red and green lights, together with our white masthead lights, illuminated the darkness. Simultaneously, at a height above us of no more than six or seven hundred feet roared a twin-engined bomber. As it did so there was a blinding flash, an impression of another, but smaller aircraft, and the roar of an igniting jet engine.

"What the hell was that?" yelled George Legge from the port wing of the bridge.

"That was a Heinkel 111," I said, "and I think it just launched a doodle-bug."

Just before dawn we were recalled to base at Gorleston where we learned that it was indeed a Heinkel which had launched the V1 weapon directly over us. This aircraft was one of several which had been specially adapted to launch the doodle-bugs in midair, thus making it possible to bring within range almost anywhere within the United Kingdom. On this particular night the designated target was Manchester, information which made me very uneasy, especially on hearing that several had succeeded in getting through the defences and reaching the area, one had actually fallen on Stockport causing casualties. Fortunately I was able to contact home and learn that my own people were safe and well.

Whether or not the intelligence services had warned of the Heinkel-launched assault on North West England on that night we never discovered. We had, however, been sent to the unusual position off the Lincolnshire coast to cover the RAF night fighters who were looking for the V1 launchers. Young Jimmy, on the stern Oerlikon, never ceased grumbling for days over the fact that if only those so-and-so's on the bridge (the skipper, George Legge and me) had told him it was a Heinkel as it approached us he would have blown it out of the sky. He probably would have done, too.

CHAPTER 19

Hard Work – but a Good Time

The summer of 1944 was a busy time. Almost every day we were sent out to rendezvous in the North Sea, from positions only twenty miles off the Norfolk coast to perilously close to the Belgian, Dutch and, on rare (but far too often) occasions, as Flight Lieutenant Lindley succinctly said, we stuck our heads into the lions mouth by venturing off the German coast itself.

In the Orderly Room someone had been reading my records and discovered that I had a driving licence. Thus it came about that on my "rest days" I found myself the driver of the small Austin van which was the one and only transport vehicle allocated to the staff of the RAF Air Sea Rescue based at the Cliff Hotel. Despite the fact that after a long and weary day at sea from early morning until late at night I was quite often dragged from my bed the following morning at 4 am to take some luckless soul being transferred to another unit the three miles to Great Yarmouth station to catch the first train out.

There were compensations in other journeys at more sociable hours to pleasanter places. Sometimes, perhaps, a little too pleasant. I remember one such occasion when I drove our Base Commanding Officer to Lowestoft for a meeting there with a friend who was in charge of a minesweeper. The reception on board was enthusiastic to say the least, and the hospitality offered to me in the crew's mess was as generous as that given to my officer in the captain's cabin.

When the decision was made to return home to Gorleston night had fallen. The distance between Lowestoft and Gorleston is about ten miles. The outward journey in daylight in the Austin van had taken thirty minutes. The return trip in the dark, no road lights at all and only the thin pencil-beams from masked headlamps took us nearly three hours. In fairness the time included several emergency stops to "empty the bilges" as my passenger expressed it. Arriving safely back at the Cliff he was fulsome in his praise of my driving expertise.

"How the devil you got us here," he said, "is a miracle. I couldn't see a damn thing all the way."

He didn't know it, but that made two of us. The only reason I even thought we *might* be on the correct road was that every time we halted to the call of nature I could hear the sea on our right-hand side, which reassured my fuddled mind that we were travelling north and eventually, with luck, would find Gorleston.

One afternoon, 2691 and its crew were stood down for the day and no request having been made for my driving services, I found myself at a loose end. For some reason I found myself thinking of a holiday I had spent with my father and a cousin at Great Yarmouth in 1936, and my holiday romance there with my very first love, Edith, a sixteen year old girl also on holiday with her parents from their home in Loughborough.

On a sunny day we met on the promenade and were immediately attracted to each other. After what we hoped was an innocuous conversation under the watchful eyes of her parents we secretly arranged to meet each other at seven o'clock the following morning in the churchyard of the parish church of St Nicholas. My excuse for my pre-breakfast excursions was that I liked to see the fishing boats off-loading their catches of the night. I never asked Edith what reason she gave to her parents, really before returning to our waiting relatives ten minutes was about all the time we had for passion and none of those precious moments could be wasted on unnecessary conversation.

She was a nice girl and although, after the holiday we never met again, we remained pen friends until, inevitably, the war changed everything and we lost contact.

Remembering this episode I had a sudden desire to go once again and see St Nicholas and its churchyard. In the eight years which had passed it didn't seem to have changed at all. I was stood looking at a tombstone by which Edith and I had our brief morning trysts and recalling that she once jokingly asked me not to press her so hard against it during our embraces as the inscription "in Loving Memory" was apt to be imprinted on her back, when a husky voice asked me "Are you looking for something, or someone?"

I found that I had an attractive ash-blonde for company. There was no better story that I could tell her but the truth, that is about Edith, I never did tell her I was a married man, although I suspect she guessed. Named Carole, her husband had been abroad with the Eighth Army for three years and she was desperately lonely. Over the next few weeks we developed a good friendship and a mutual respect for each other. She was a very patient girl, more often than not I did not appear at the time or place we had arranged to meet, the ever-changing demands of the Air Sea Rescue service saw to that. She was not on the telephone either at her home or work so if I were suddenly detailed for a not previously specified duty there was no way I could notify her. We would make three dates at the same rendezvous and hope that by the third one at worse I would appear.

This system worked until the last occasion when, unexpectedly, I was transferred to another unit. I had missed the first of our next arranged meeting and could imagine her disappointment and possibly tears, when I never appeared at the next two. She must have thought that I had grown tired of her and decided to end the affair. Such was not the case, but she had refused to give me her home address and there was no way I could contact her.

Nevertheless, I was far from happy with myself.

Some Were Lucky

CHAPTER 20

Stolen Glory

During August 1944 we were at sea most days. The weather was, in the main, fine and dry but more often than not there was a stiff westerly wind blowing which made for a choppy sea and uncomfortable conditions, rolling about when we were lying-to at our rendezvous positions. Being the better sailor of the two "Pinto" was content to spend his time in the wireless cabin whilst I lodged myself in the starboard corner of the bridge. In the headset I wore one earphone allowed me to listen to the radio traffic and the other one was connected to the boat's intercom system.

Despite it being summer, and wearing a thick woollen sweater under my duffel coat, it could be desperately cold. Returning to harbour at dusk, having been out since daybreak, I had stiff limbs and a face white with salt from the sea spray. However, a hot bath and a good meal at the Cliff soon put me right again.

The beginning of September brought a welcome break when HSL2691 was ordered to make the short journey down the coast, through the harbour at Lowestoft and in to Oulton Broad. Here she was hauled up a slipway for examination and cleaning of the below water section of her hull. Despite the fact that she was less than six months old she had a surprising amount of marine growth attached to her which was detrimental to her speed. Two days hard work by the shipyard workers made her as good as new, and as fast as she had ever been – something which was to very soon pay dividends.

As so often happens in early autumn the winds eased, the days were fine and warm, and the sea calm. The bombing of enemy-held territory continued unabated, by the RAF at night and the US Army Airforce by day. Together with our old Weymouth colleague, HSL2707 and several Royal Navy ML's, we formed a chain of rescue boats stretching out at ten mile intervals to over eighty miles from the English coast.

Some ten days after the sojourn at Oulton Broad we were sent out one morning to cover bombing missions by formations of Flying Fortresses. The allotted rendezvous for 2691 was in the number three position, which meant that there were two launches nearer to Germany than ourselves, although we were fairly close to the Frisian Islands. By mid-afternoon the sun was shining down out of a cloudless blue sky and the sea was as smooth as a sheet of glass. It was that rarity in the North Sea – a hot day.

So hot that I had taken off my duffel coat and battledress top. I was alone on the bridge. Over the last few weeks there had been no reported encounters with either enemy aircraft or E-boats and we were growing complacent. The crew, even Jimmy (the Oerlikon) and George Legge had gone below. Some were playing cards on the table in the mess deck, others dozing in the sickbay, whilst the skipper was enjoying the Spartan comforts of his tiny cabin. In the wheelhouse "Chiefy" was doing his best to keep his eyes open as we drifted gently round and round our buoy. So placid was the sea that for hours it had not been necessary to run the engines to creep back up to it and maintain position. The two Geordie engineers were lying on the aft deck sunbathing. The war was a long way away.

Alone on the bridge I was not finding it easy to keep awake. It was undoubtedly my earlier training for aircrew which kept mentally insisting that the greatest possibility of danger was when it was least expected. Consequently I kept myself alert by walking from one side of the bridge to the other and never staying still for more than a couple of minutes in any one position. This state of affairs had been going on for some time when I became aware of the faint noise of aircraft engines. Picking up the skipper's binoculars, which he had left lying by the compass I scanned the sky in the direction of the sound. Seconds later, very low over the water, coming towards us from the east and trailing smoke, was a Flying Fortress.

I pressed the alarm button and the strident clamour of ringing bells brought the skipper and crew scrambling up the companionway. "Chiefy," now fully awake, was already ringing for the engines as our two Geordie mechanics tumbled out of sight down their hatchway like rabbits into their burrow with a ferret after them. Possibly they had visions of a repetition of the D-Day episode. No explanation from me was required, the emergency was all too apparent. No more than fifty feet above the sea, and only about a hundred yards away, the Fortress came thundering by us as our engines started. I fired the colours of the day from the Very pistol to assure the bomber that we were friendly, as 2691 gained way and "Chiefy" brought the launch round on to a course following the crippled bomber.

It was quite a chase. All the time we were working up to maximum speed the Fortress, skimming the surface of the water, was rapidly going away from us. It had become a mere dot disappearing over the horizon when, suddenly, the trail of smoke abruptly ceased and, although by this time we must have been lagging behind at least seven miles rising in the air, a column of water was clearly visible.

"He's down," yelled Lindley, binoculars to his eyes, "can't see a damn thing though!"

That was understandable. Engines at full throttle HSL2691 was roaring over the water faster than she had ever done before. Calm though the conditions were, the launch was bounding along like a demented kangaroo, making it impossible to accurately visually focus on one spot for more than a few seconds at a time.

For the next minute or two we rocketed along on the same heading, hoping that we would be able to find survivors. We were lucky. We did.

A small dot on the surface of the sea grew larger as we came nearer. It was an inflated rubber dinghy, and crowded with men. If weather conditions had not been so good the dinghy would never have been unable to support so many. There were nine of them, wearing their Mae West life jackets, eight sitting in the circle of the dinghy with their arms interlocked, leaving just enough room for the remaining one to be sat in the centre. Despite the calm sea water was already slopping over the rim of their orange-coloured lifeboat, and if we had not reached them so quickly they could have been in serious trouble.

Quickly assessing the situation the skipper reduced our speed to a crawl and "Chiefy" carefully manoeuvred the launch so that it came gently alongside the dinghy. One by one the American airmen were carefully lifted aboard. With the exception of one of the waist gunners who had a bullet wound in his left leg, no other member of the Fortress's crew were injured.

As this was being done we became aware of another craft coming towards us at high speed from the west. Although the gunners were alerted we were not unduly alarmed as any surface vessel approaching from this direction was almost certain to be friendly. Sure enough as it came nearer it was identified as a Royal Navy ML, the boat allocated the number four position (nearer to England than ourselves) on that particular day.

Closing to within a few hundred yards the ML reduced speed and began to circle round us. There was a blast of Morse in my headset as the Navy boat called base. They were really upset because, breaking all the rules, their message was not coded but in plain language. It will not be recorded for posterity as was Nelson's at Trafalgar, but nevertheless warrants a small place in history, at least for the RAF.

The signal read : "HSL2691 has pinched my bomber!"

As we learned later, the Flying Fortress, was being "homed" (directed) to the ML in the hope that a successful emergency landing might be made on the sea close by. Well, the aircraft did not quite make it that far, and we had arrived at the point of "ditching" within minutes, much to the chagrin of the Navy boys who were still some miles away. Their feelings must have been even further hurt when Base, responding to their signal, ordered the ML to take over the original position of 2691, who was to return to harbour and land the survivors.

That was one instruction we obeyed with alacrity.

Below deck "Doc" had treated the wounded gunner and, aided by some of the deck hands, made certain that the rest of the bomber crew's clothes were dried out and that they were none the worse for their ordeal. Purely for medicinal purposes, of course, generous tots of rum had driven away the danger of anyone catching a chill.

It was not very long before the captain of the Fortress came up to the bridge. A very grateful Lieutenant Tetreault, of the US Army Airforce, his squadron operated from Rattlesden airfield in Cambridgeshire.

"They always tell us at briefing that if ever we come down in the sea that you boys are quick off the mark," he said, "but I never believed you were as sharp as that! We hardly got our feet wet. The folks back home will be mighty impressed when they get to hear about this!"

Home, I think, was California. The Lieutenant, like the other members of his crew, would be about twenty years old.

We were just coming up to the Smith's Knoll buoy when another of the Americans joined us on the bridge.

"Gee," he exclaimed, looking over the bridge screen, "what a wonderful sight! I've always wanted to see that."

All I could see ahead was the flat, brown coastline of Norfolk.

"What is it?" I asked.

"Surely," he replied, "you can see them."

"See what?"

"The white cliffs of Dover. Ain't they just a grand sight!"

We never knew what particular role he fulfilled in the Fortress's crew, but we all agreed he would have made an fitting navigator for our own first skipper, "Plum" Field.

Some Were Lucky

CHAPTER 21

The Western Isles

Not all calls to assist "ditching" aircraft were successful. On so many occasions we searched a given area for many hours without finding any trace of them or their crew. But we always assiduously carried out a "square search". Simply explained, on reaching the designated area, this meant steering one mile north, then one mile east, one mile south and one mile west to bring us back to the original starting point. The operation was then repeated on an adjoining "box" position. This could go on ad infinitum – the sea is a big and lonely place.

Only once did we have any success. Although a miracle it was still a disappointment. We were on the final leg of one of the "boxes" when we sighted a lone figure struggling in the sea. The scrambling net was thrown over the side and as we edged carefully up to the Mae West supported struggler two of the deck hands leaned over and plucked him out of the water.

There was a disgusted yell of "Throw him back, he's one of ours!"

He was. It was our own medical orderly, "Doc" Deakin, who had been snoozing in the sunshine on the after-deck and had slid overboard as we turned 90 degrees on the next leg of the search. It took a long time for him to live this down – but actually he was a very lucky man that we should retrace our course exactly over the spot in which he was floundering.

As the summer of 1944 came to an end so did my days on HSL2691. Six months, apparently, was deemed to be the maximum serving time in the job I had been doing, after that the theory was that efficiency would deteriorate. The first I knew of an impending move was when, returning to harbour at Gorleston one evening after a particularly rough, unpleasant and unsuccessful trip, my replacement was sat waiting on the quayside.

I must confess that, although regretting parting with the many friends I had made, I was not sorry to be missing the forthcoming North Sea winter weather.

Luckily the long journey to my new posting was broken by having seven days leave at home. It also gave me the opportunity to look at a map and find out where I was going. *Tiree*? "Somewhere in the Hebrides" was all that the Gorleston Orderly Room could tell me. "No idea what goes on there, but we expect you'll find out. Get to Oban and it'll either be a long swim, or if you're lucky there might be a ferry."

Travel by rail had not improved after five years of war. The first stage from Norfolk to home with the prospect of seeing my family, was bearable despite taking over twenty-four hours with three changes on route, but once my leave was over the journey onwards seemed to take for ever. Spending a whole night on a blacked-out station platform in Glasgow waiting for a connection to Oban certainly did not help. However, on arrival there my luck was in. There **was** a ferry...

It was a fine, sunny morning when the steamer sailed. A brisk westerly wind blew away any cobwebs remaining from the trauma of my travels on the railway. Crossing the Firth of Lorne and entering the Sound of Mull the majestic splendour of the island of that name came into view on the port side.

Tobermory was the first port of call. In a beautiful bay, the small town is sheltered from the worst of the Atlantic weather by the towering hills around it and enjoys an extremely temperate climate for a location so far North. Watching the bustle on the quayside as stores from the mainland were unloaded it was easy to visualise the relief of the crew of one of the fleeing galleons of the Spanish Armada when, after surviving the perils of Pentland Firth and Cape Wrath, they found shelter here.

Leaving Tobermory the ferry dipped her bows as the first of the Atlantic rollers made their presence felt. The next call was the Isle of Coll, where, from the few scattered dwellings constituting the village Arinagour, a diesel-engined fishing boat came out to meet us. With immaculate timing, sacks containing (I believed) mail, and possibly supplies of not too fragile a nature, were flung from the steamer on to her deck. With equal dexterity a bearded member of the fishing boat's crew flung back a sack of their own. I could only hope that whatever might have been in it there were no eggs! What I did not realise is that I was, personally, soon to receive similar treatment.

Coll was a dramatic change from the hills and lush vegetation of Mull, being a totally flat and featureless strip of land, nowhere it seemed, rising more than some twenty feet above sea level. Approaching Tiree it became evident that similar conditions prevailed. I was engrossed in considering this when the ship's loud-hailer, in a braw Scottish accent demanded my attention.

"Will the airman for Tiree go midships starboard side with all his kit – now!"

Over four years in the Air Force had taught me to obey orders without question. Emulating a certain story of the Christian Bible I picked my gear and went.

I was met by one of the ferry's crew.

"That your kitbag?" he asked.

I nodded.

"That's no problem," he said, "but what about that lot?"

The lot to which he referred happened to be my backpack, which contained the majority of my gear and personnel possessions. I told him so.

He reflectively stroked his beard and came to a decision.

"Well, it's up to you. In a few minutes we'll be at Scarinish. That's the landing place for Tiree. Sometimes we can tie up at the jetty, but not today. The swell is too much. So we'll toss your kitbag ashore, and you can jump after it. Mind you if you miss and fall in the 'oggin with that lot on your back it could be some time before we see you again. Reckon the skipper won't be wanting to wait that long."

I took the hint and took off the backpack.

"Very good," he nodded graciously, "when I say jump, you jump. I'll throw this lot after you."

And that's the way it happened. The ferry came broadside to the jetty, rolling sickenly as she moved slowly ahead with fenders out some four feet away. On an up-roll my guiding star yelled "Jump!" I jumped and much to my relief landed safely ashore, albeit on my hands and knees. Rising to my feet to thank him for his assistance I was promptly knocked back on my knees by the arrival of a kitbag, and totally flattened when, seconds later, a heavy backpack made a crash-landing on my shoulders.

Gasping for breath, and struggling upright once again, I became aware of the presence of a gentleman bearing the two stripes of a corporal on his sleeve. Even in my bemused state he impressed me as the scruffiest RAF NCO it had, so far, been my pleasure to meet.

"You made it, then," he said without a great deal of obvious pleasure, "one of these days someone won't."

The journey to the airfield, in a somewhat dilapidated small van which complemented its driver's appearance, took only a few minutes. Not surprising as Tiree is ten miles in length and, at its widest point, about four miles. The island was totally devoid of vegetation, not a tree, nor shrub and as flat as the proverbial pancake. The prevailing strong westerly winds were responsible for that. They also ensured that, of all the airfields in the United Kingdom, conditions for safe takeoffs and landings, were generally acceptable when elsewhere they were impossible. This was essential for the purposes of the squadron based there.

The aircraft were four-engined Halifax bombers, specially adapted for meteorological reconnaissance flights. Their missions were to fly out almost halfway across the Atlantic, heights varying at planned points from 18,000 feet down to sea level, reporting wind speeds and direction together with barometric pressures. This information was vital in forecasting the European climatic conditions and the planning of all Allied operations.

Whilst the so-called "weather" crews did not have to brave enemy flak and fighters their job was equally as dangerous. In snow, thunderstorms, gales......whatever the weather they flew. Navigation had to be absolutely accurate, there was no room for error, and when a descent from maximum height down to sea level was called for, often through dense cloud and in total darkness, nerves must have been at screaming pitch. In my time on the island there was only one fatal accident. That was when a Halifax, taking off, charged down the runway at full throttle, and had barely reached an altitude of two hundred feet when an incoming Halifax emerged from the low cloud and they met head-on. There were no survivors.

My own work was the maintenance, calibration and testing of the aircraft radio equipment. It was interesting enough, especially when the aircrew wireless operators discovered that I had also once been a member of their fraternity. That was, by now, over two years before. In wartime – literally – a lifetime. Perhaps the occasions I enjoyed most was when I was detailed for the night emergency duty. There I was, all on my own, in a Nissen hut and surrounded with radio equipment. Every morning, about 2 am appeared a mouse. At first he was very wary of me but, after a few weeks became very bold. Whenever I unwrapped my issued refreshments, usually sandwiches the contents of which defied identification, he would appear in front of me. Obviously, I called him Mickey. I valued his friendship. If he would eat the crumbs I offered him then the sandwiches were, possibly, fit for human consumption.

At Tiree all accommodation was in Nissen huts. Because of the constant strong westerly winds the concrete paths between the huts had ropes aligned for personnel to grip as they made they way around the site to avoid being blown into the morass of the surrounding swampy terrain.

It took some time, but eventually I came to love Tiree. There was nothing nicer, when not on duty, than to stand, at dusk on the beach outside my own Nissen hut on the shores of Hynish Bay and, as the sun appeared to sink into the sea, look at the distant golden outlines of the islands of Mull, Jura and Islay.

The base had its own small orchestra, six peacetime professional musicians. They were very good and entertained all ranks on an equal basis, playing in turn in the Officer's Mess one night, the next in the Sergeant's and then the Naafi. Occasionally they played at a station Dance Night. These were not too successful as out of the 2,000 RAF personnel only about 100 were female, and the local young ladies, attractive as they were, could only add about a dozen more. The general "moan" was – all these men, so few women, and only 500 sheep.

The band also gave polish to the station concert party shows. These were held in the camp cinema which had a good stage. There was a wealth of talent available, singers, comedians and even two magicians and a juggler. Shows were produced about every six weeks. The programmes carried the message "New Members Welcome," so I filled in the application to join. After what I thought had been quite a successful audition, in which I demonstrated my prowess as a stand-up comedian, ending the act in my dulcet tones with a sentimental ballad, I was accepted ——— as a scene-shifter!

However, a little later, this turned out to be an important appointment.

Along came May, 1945, and the end of the war in Europe. To me it was something of an anticlimax. After, through no choice of my own, being involved more than most in the thick of things, it seemed a little unfair to be on a Hebridean island far away from the celebrations taking place on the mainland. Still, I supposed it was better then being out in India or Burma.

I should have known better.

The Western Isles

RAF Air Sea Rescue Launch

Some Were Lucky

CHAPTER 22

A Short Hop, and a Long Voyage

The war in Europe had ended, but for week after week the work of the meteorological squadron continued. It seemed that nothing would ever change, but suddenly it did.

The squadron was given a movement order. The first we of the ground crew knew about it was one evening when we were ordered to pack our kit and be ready to move the next morning. This time it was not my luck to have the pleasure of a leisurely cruise on the island ferry, but a draughty, uncomfortable flight in the bomb bay of a Liberator. Fortunately the journey was of only an hour's duration, southwards to Northern Ireland and Aldergrove airfield.

Located about twelve miles west of Belfast, and on the shores of Lough Neagh, during the war Aldergrove had been one of Coastal Command's most important bases and had played an active, and successful, role in the Battle of the Atlantic.

Compared to conditions on Tiree accommodation was luxurious and we quickly settled in. The number of hours flown by the Halifaxes on their weather missions began to ease off and we had more leisure time on our hands. The RAF band had stayed behind on Tiree, and the numbers of the concert party had been reduced by the loss of the non-squadron personnel who also had not moved to Northern Ireland. This gave me my big chance. I was promoted from stagehand to be an actual member of the cast! Rehearsals for the forthcoming show were well under way when the hammer blow fell.

One morning I was instructed to report to the Orderly Room. "Ah," said the corporal on duty, "I have news for you. Some good, some not so good." He peered at me benignly over his RAF issue spectacles. "We'll have the good news first. This afternoon you are going on leave."

My heart sank, I could guess what was coming.

"The not-so good bit is, that afterwards you are going out East. Seems the invasion of Japan is awaiting your appearance on the scene there." He smiled at me encouragingly. "Now, don't be modest and say they can manage it without you, because I'm sure the powers-that-be won't make a move unless they have you behind them."

Father and Son, Bryan, at home on leave 1945

Beyond muttering that the further I was behind everybody else the better I would like it there was nothing I could do. Once again packing all my gear I caught the night ferry from Belfast to Heysham and spent the next ten days at home with my wife and family. My son Bryan was now more than two years old. So far in his young life we had seen very little of each other, I felt extremely despondent when I left for the Wirral and the West Kirby camp to await embarkation from Liverpool.

The news of Hiroshima and the atom bomb came the following day, closely followed by a second bomb at Nagasaki and the capitulation of Japan a few days later.

A wave of optimism immediately swept the camp. Surely there would be no possibility of putting hundreds of people on a ship to sail thousands of miles to a war which no longer existed. We eagerly scanned the notice boards for fresh instructions.

There weren't any.

Plans for systematic demobilisation of the armed forces at the end of hostilities had been planned and publicised for some time, for which a combination of age and length of service resulted in a number being allocated to every individual. Mine was 32. The end of the war in Europe in May 1945 had already seen those personnel classified up to the early 'teens being sent back to "civvy street." I was reasonably confident that within a few weeks I, too, would be going home for good.

Several more days went by during which the notice boards were scanned as they had never been before. Then, one evening, like wildfire, a rumour spread through the camp that a new batch of "demob numbers" up to 24 had been promulgated.

There were howls of rage the next morning when, at last, the notice boards had news for us. Transportation to Wellington Dock, Liverpool, had been arranged for the following day for all whose names were listed. Eventually pushing my way through to the front of a seething mob of airmen I anxiously scanned the columns of the hundreds of names. Sure enough, under the "G's," was mine, and with the correct service number. So there was no mistake.

That evening there were impromptu protest meetings held in the huts and the Naafi at which threats of various forms of mutiny, such as refusing to get on to the lorries to Liverpool, or walking out of the camp and going home. The suggestion which brought the loudest roars of approval was to kidnap the Station Warrant Officer (nearly always the most unpopular character in any camp) and hold him hostage until the Air Ministry cancelled any plans to send us overseas.

In the event, we all paraded as instructed, boarded the lorries, and off we went to the dock.

There awaited us the troopship "Scythia," a converted pre-war Atlantic liner of some 22,000 tons. As on my previous ship to North Africa I was allocated a hammock below deck, sharing accommodation with some two hundred other airmen. I was told that there were over 2,000 souls aboard, soldiers, sailors, airmen – and some girls – members of all three services. I never saw them. They were (quite rightly) kept to the upper decks.

The voyage itself, compared to the 1943 experience on the "Duchess of York," was uneventful and, in most respects, even enjoyable. The war over convoys had been discontinued and the "Scythia" sailed alone. As we left the dock in Liverpool and steamed down the river towards the sea, the Mersey ferries saluted us with their sirens and the people aboard them waved their farewells and shouted their good wishes across the widening intervening water.

It was almost worth going..............

No. **It wasn't**.

I remember looking at the coast of North Wales as dusk was falling. The "Scythia" picked up speed and began to pitch to the rising sea in the freshening wind. My mind went back to the last time I had seen this coastline in similar fashion. It was when I was a boy, on holiday, sailing with my father from Liverpool to Llandudno on what I then thought was the greatest ship in the world, the "St. Tudno." It was probably only one-tenth the size of the troopship I was on.

The Bay of Biscay lived up to its reputation for gales and rough seas making the first four days thoroughly miserable for most of those on board. As we neared the entrance to the Mediterranean the skies cleared, the heaving grey sea turned into a placid blue and we sailed past Gibraltar in warm sunshine. It was certainly very different from over two years before when the "Duchess of York," and the North African convoy, had stolen through the Straits in the dead of night. Even stranger was sailing towards, and then past, Malta without fear of attack. If it had taken some time before we became inured to the rigours of war. It seemed it might take us longer before we could live easily with peace.

Only whilst the "Scythia" was lying in the harbour at Port Said, awaiting her turn to pass into the Suez Canal, were the rumours that we were going to Indonesia corrected by the official announcement of our destination – Bombay, India. Although no one had the slightest idea what we were meant to do in India, there was some comfort in the fact that we were not going to be as far away from home as we had previously thought.

Sailing through the Canal was interesting enough, if uncomfortably hot, and it was a relief when we emerged at Suez into the Red Sea. Relief which was short-lived, for as the ship proceeded southward towards Aden the temperature rose higher and higher until conditions aboard the crowded trooper became almost unbearable. Even the interminable card schools came to a halt.

Crossing the Indian Ocean the weather cooled sufficiently enough to encourage speculation that, on reaching Bombay, the "Scythia" would simply turn around and take us all back to the UK. The war was over and India had been promised independence, there could not possibly be anything for us to do there.

Once again we were to be proved wrong. As the tugs were busily assisting the troopship into her berth so the duty lists began to appear on the notice boards. On one of the first appeared my own name, and against it instructions to proceed to New Delhi and report there to the Headquarters Signals Section. I collected a travel warrant from the ship's Orderly Office and, laden down with all my kit, together with four other similarly unfortunate airmen were taken through the dusty streets and teeming crowds to the railway station.

Some Were Lucky

CHAPTER 23

New Delhi

The rail journey from Bombay to New Delhi took just over twenty-four hours. There were six of us in our party, all RAF personnel, and we were lucky to have a first class compartment to ourselves. The seats were extremely hard and uncomfortable. Shared with the occupants next door, was a toilet which was even more so. Under the seats were steel boxes which, we were told, contained ice – a primitive form of air conditioning. We were given stern warnings not to be tempted to open the boxes and suck any of the ice. If we did, we would almost certainly contact cholera and be dead within a few hours. Whether this was true, or not, we never knew – but the boxes were not opened.

If the first class accommodation was somewhat primitive conditions elsewhere on the train defy description. Hauled along by two engines, most of the time, and sixteen carriages in length, every compartment was crammed full of humanity. Those who could not squeeze into the carriages clung precariously to the running boards, or perched even more dangerously on the roofs. There were hundreds of them. Amazingly none of them as – far as we were aware – ever fell, or were knocked off as we trundled along. At every station the number of passengers increased, for every one who alighted it seemed that another ten climbed on board.

The only sustenance we had were the ration packs given to us when leaving Bombay. These were those issued to all personnel serving where no established catering facilities existed and consisted of a tin of corned beef, another of spam, three hard biscuits, a small chocolate bar and some foul-tasting unidentified tablets which were guaranteed to protect us from most health-threatening hazards. As Taffy Jones, my particular friend in the party said, undoubtedly these tablets were also a deterrent to ghouls and vampires too.

To keep our thirst at bay we had our water bottles, from which we drank sparingly as we were wary of re-filling them at any of the stops along the route. At many of the stations refreshing cups of tea were available from the local "char wallah" who would make a beeline for the carriages containing Europeans and the surety of profitable sales. Nevertheless, he was a welcome sight with his containers of steaming liquid hanging from the yoke across his shoulders. We were glad to see him during the dry dusty heat of the day, but even more so during the dark cold hours of night when we wondered if we were on a never-ending journey to nowhere. Eventually came the dawn, the promise of yet another hot day, and breakfast saw the consumption of the, by now repulsive, last morsels of our ration packs.

Mid-morning and we arrived at New Delhi. The journey had seemed interminable. It was a surprise to have arrived there at all, and an even bigger one awaited us in the form of an RAF lorry to transport us to our quarters – it appeared that someone was expecting us.

The base to which we were taken was located near the racecourse and consisted of a number of bungalows, each of which accommodated twelve airmen. After the voyage on the troopship and our experiences since landing in India, our quarters were comparatively luxurious. The sense of wellbeing was further heightened by the Indians employed there. A personal servant, known as a bearer, was allocated to look after every three men. We each paid our bearer, his name was Sofi, a princely sum in annas which, in today's UK money, amounted to something like 7½ pence per week. For that he was loyal and trustworthy, made our beds, polished our buttons and shoes, and kept our part of the room clean and tidy. He also did his best to teach us Hindustani but his mastery of the English language was always far superior to our efforts to speak his native tongue.

New Delhi 1945

Whilst there were no strict rules that I was ever aware of, the Indians had there own code of discipline. Only the bearers ever came into our bungalow. The "char wallah" with his two urns of tea slung over his shoulders on a wooden yoke came by outside at frequent intervals, offering his wares in a high-pitched chant. The "dhobi wallah" appeared daily in the doorway bringing back the clean laundry and taking away the next load of washing. By the gate of the compound sat the "pump wallah," patiently waiting with his bicycle pump and hoping somebody would ask for air in their bicycle tyres. Unfortunately this type of transport was very scarce at that time, so he was never very busy. Every morning as I left on my twenty minute walk up the broad flower-lined avenue to the RAF Headquarters his liquid brown eyes met mine as if imploring me to get a bicycle so that he could blow up my tyres. Like all Indians he had a fierce pride, rejecting my offers of a few annas charity when he could do nothing for me in return. After some weeks we reached a compromise. At breakfast I would slip a roll of bread in my pocket and hand it to him as I walked past. I learned later that he would proudly take it as a contribution to his family's food in the shanty he knew as home.

In 1945 nationalistic feelings were running high in the subcontinent, and the calls for independence from British rule incessant. Despite this I never experienced any personal hostility from the Indians with whom I had any contact. Sofi, who was a keen member of one of the political factions, would say, "Sahib, no leave the camp tonight, big demonstration in the city. We all shout "Jai Hind!" (Quit India). "No trouble if you are not there!" We took his advice, and there was never any trouble. Most nights the city was calm and peaceful and the shopkeepers and traders only too anxious to please and take our money off us. They certainly had an eye for business. Confident of the forthcoming end of British rule, souvenirs of our stay in India were for sale everywhere. I bought some attractive enamelled ornaments which I thought to be epitomes of Indian craft. They certainly were. When I later examined them in the brighter lights of the camp, stamped on the back of each piece was, "Made in Birmingham."

It was November 1945. Whatever the reason why I, and a few thousand others like me, had been sent out to India at this time remained a mystery. Every morning I reported to the Communications Officer of the Day and, after exchanging pleasantries with him and any other bored airmen hanging around made my way to the canteen for sufficient coffee and biscuits to hold body and soul together until lunchtime. It therefore came as a shock when one day I was summoned to appear before the august presence of the Base Commanding Officer. Luckily the "dhobi wallah" had just delivered a complete outfit of newly washed and pressed uniform so, with the help of the faithful Sofi, who meticulously made sure that my campaign medal ribbons were in the correct order, I duly presented myself before the great man.

"Ah, Goodwin," he said, "Just the man we've been looking for."

This was not a good start to the proceedings. Only once had I ever volunteered for anything – and that was over six years before. Since then I had had plenty of time to reflect on my rashness. Surely at this stage of the proceedings they were not looking for heroes for a suicide mission. Or were they?

There was only one answer I could give to his opening remark.

"Sir!" I responded.

The Group Captain shuffled through some papers on his desk. "Er – um," he continued, "I see you've had a more interesting war than most, eh?"

I had never been one to argue with authority. "Possibly, sir, but I was rather hoping that now, perhaps, the RAF could carry on without me and I could go home."

"All in good time, my boy, all in good time." He studied one of the sheets of paper in front of him for what seemed ages, but what was possibly only thirty seconds, whilst I feverishly wondered which of my past misdemeanours had finally come to roost.

The Group Captain, having finally digested the information in front of him, looked up at me.

"Goodwin," he said, "it says here that you have stage experience."

"Pardon?"

"Stage experience – acting, singing, dancing – all that sort of thing."

"Not me, sir, honest, never. My mother used to sing............."

"I'm not talking about your mother, I'm talking about you. It says here, in your records, that *you* have stage experience. Records are never wrong, well, very rarely. So *that* is *that!*"

"Yes sir. Do Records say where I had this experience?"

"Of course! On an island called Tiree. Where the devil is that, out in the Pacific somewhere?"

"No sir. As a matter of fact it is part of the Hebridean islands of Scotland. My stage experience there was as a scene-shifter for the RAF station concert party. Sorry, sir, but other than that I have no thespian qualifications."

"We're talking about performing, not some thespian whatever trade union thing. That's not allowed in the services anyway. Just let's stick to the matter in hand, shall we?"

"Yes, sir," I said, wishing to heaven that I knew what it was.

"Now that the war is over there are thousands of airmen and soldiers in the Delhi area who, like you want to go home. There's nothing much to do, and we've more than outstayed our welcome with the Indians. Consequently morale is not quite what it should be. I am going to do something about that – starting now – and starting with you Goodall!"

"Goodwin, sir"

"We're going to have a stage show, a jolly good stage show and we have a good stage here on which to produce it. You, Goodwin or whatever your name is, are going to do exactly that!"

"Pardon?"

"Money is no object, shouldn't cost too much anyway. There must be some talent amongst all these idle bodies around the country. So stop being one of them and get cracking straight away."

"Sir, I really don't have any qualifications to do what you want......."

"You've told me your mother was an actress, or singer or something, and your records state that you've had stage experience yourself. It must run in the blood, that's good enough for me. Also, Records can't find anyone else in this part of the world with any experience at all. So the job is yours, and you start now."

"Now, Sir?"

"Again, according to Records, you have one or two defects. Deafness isn't one of them. There is an office down the corridor allocated to you. I shall pop in from time to time to see how you are getting on. Don't even dream of going home to England until we've had the best stage show ever produced for the Forces in this part of the world. Remember it had better be humorous as well, our aim is to boost morale."

That concluded the interview. Certainly my morale, which previously hadn't been all that bad, now needed a boost very badly. Locating the office allocated was simple, it had a large notice on the door which proclaimed in large letters "Entertainments Section." I opened the door to discover a recumbent figure, wreathed in tobacco smoke and sprawled in one of the only two chairs in the room, with his feet on the desk.

"Hi," he said, "welcome to the club. I assume you're the unfortunate lad given such a wonderful opportunity to make a name for yourself – one way or another. Not to worry, as your chief assistant I'll make sure you don't come to too much harm. My name is Bennet, just call me Ben, and I've been allocated to help because I'm the best scrounger in the whole of the South East Asia Command. Just say what you want and I'll get it for you."

As he stood up and held out his hand I realised that he was a Warrant Officer.

Noting my surprise he quickly put me at ease. "You're the boss," he said, "forget the difference in rank. I'm sure we'll get along fine."

We did. In the weeks we worked together Ben was an indefatigable worker. Nothing was ever too much trouble and, true to his word, whatever I asked for he got from somewhere. Wisely I never queried from where or how.

Announcements on the local Forces radio, appeals on canteen and unit notice boards brought in a flood of applicants for auditions. After some three weeks during which Ben and I suffered the tortures of listening to off-key tenors, budding Bing Crosbys and muddled magicians we had sufficient talent to start rehearsals. In addition to the twelve airmen we had selected we had also the great fortune to have from the women's services six very attractive girls two of them with good singing voices and the others with considerable dancing ability, both ballet and tap.

So, I had a cast, but no idea what I wanted them to do.

As with all my other problems Ben quickly found the solution. He simply asked them all what they would like to do best and within hours ideas were pouring in. A remark that we all must be suffering from some sort of mania gave us the title of the show – "Stage Mania." Blatantly we adapted the tune of "Pennsylvania Polka" as the opening number. At the beginning of the show the twelve men walked in front of the main curtain singing :

"Strike up the music the band has begun
To play the opening chorus
Pull back the curtain and bring the girls on
We hope you're rooting for us........."

On the nights of the show the audience certainly were. 99.9% of them were men, most of whom hadn't seen a female form in such revealing dress for over four years. It was the only time I ever saw Ben worried. The term "minder" hadn't been invented then, but he had the right idea in having a number of the RAF's equivalent of military police (Service Police) positioned in the wings just in case..........

Strangely enough this gave us the idea of what was to become one of our most popular sketches, or more accurately perhaps, a mini comic opera. The scene was an RAF court martial and opened with two S.P.'s singing to the tune of "Les Beaux Gendarmes"

"We are the black sheep of the service as you all no doubt agree,
For there's nothing quite so lowering as to be a RAF S.P..."

This always brought the house down and the success of the sketch was assured.

"Stage Mania" was a very popular show and held the stage for a full week plus a three day repetition some few weeks later. The Base Commanding Officer came to the first night of the show. Ben told me that he seemed pleased, and somewhat relieved, so we wondered who had been leaning on *him*. I never saw him again, but he must have been grateful because a few days after the final curtain came down came my orders to return home to the UK.

I was very sorry to leave Ben. A regular serviceman himself he did his best to persuade me to stay in New Delhi and sign on in the RAF for a period of at least a further seven years. With the contacts we had made through the show he reckoned that together we could make a fortune. I had a wife and young son, now three years old, whom I had hardly seen. So, I said no, I wanted to go home.

Ben said I was a fool, the world was my oyster. He might have been right – I'll never know.

CHAPTER 24

Over and Out

"All my life, sahib, I have been a believer that the British must leave India so that we could rule ourselves and be a great nation. Now you are starting to go, and I wonder what we will do without you. If I cannot work here at the camp what else is there for me to do? When you have all gone who is going to give rupees, or even annas, to Sofi to help feed and clothe the family?"

It was a very doleful Sofi to whom I said goodbye in that May of 1946. I have often wondered how he, and the many hundreds of thousands like him, have fared in life. Well, I hope, because I never met a nicer man.

The journey from Delhi by train back to Bombay was a repetition of the outward trip seven months before, but this time, having had some experience of the country, its climate and its people, not the ordeal it had been before. Waiting at the station was an open-topped lorry – transport to the docks. Our documents having been checked by a worried and overtired officer sporting the familiar red armband of the RAF Service Police we were handed over to the mercies of an extremely cheerful Indian driver. Any ideas we had of saying a dignified nostalgic farewell to the subcontinent were rapidly dispelled as we clung desperately to whatever support we could find as with a screaming engine, alternating with screeching brakes, our driver weaved his way through the teeming streets of the city. Miraculously we not only arrived at the dock but stopped before going over the edge into the water. There, before us, and looking enormous tied up alongside, was our ship for home.

"Andes" was her name. By wartime standards she was brand new, having been built, I believe in the late 1930's for the Royal Mail line and – as her name indicates designed for the UK – South America trade. She was also reputed to be extremely fast. We were told her cruising speed was in excess of 20 knots, so we congratulated ourselves as extremely fortunate to have her to take us home. Accommodation was as on all troopships at that time, officers cramped in the few upper-deck cabins and other ranks in even greater discomfort in hammocks slung touching each other in the decks below. There were even more occupants of these quarters than at first we realised. After less than an hour on board we were all itching and scratching as voraciously hungry lice and fleas welcomed new supplies of food. On complaining we were informed that to delouse the ship would mean, at best, a delay in sailing of at least a week and, at worst, total unloading of the ship and spending an unspecified time in a transit camp ashore until other transport became available. Enquiries established that the "Andes" previous mission had been to transport native troops to Indonesia. Apparently they were accustomed to insect friends. If they could tolerate it, so would we, it was decided.

The "Andes" sailed on time from Bombay into the setting sun, in addition to her crew she had on board some 1500 "demob happy" service personnel and a few million contented well-fed lice and fleas.

Compared to my previous troopship voyages the "Andes" was a luxury cruise. She was a fast ship, the trip from Bombay to Southampton taking only eleven days – very rapid transport for those days. Although I was unaware of it at the time the progress of homeward-bound troopships was chartered on a huge map in the Public Library in my home town of Stockport. Here, my dear old mother used to eagerly watch the pins representing the whereabouts of the ships returning from the Far East as they made their way to the UK.

To complicate matters (and she was a born worrier) there were two ships reported sailing with RAF personnel on board from India. The "Georgic" and the "Andes." The first was scheduled to dock in Liverpool and the latter at Southampton – both on the same day. Mother was wonderful at improvisation, but even she couldn't cope with that! She could only watch the display in the library and hope that when those pins were finally placed on the map in the two British ports her little boy would have returned home safely from the war. Every day my wife, Nora, living in the nearby village of Poynton, would get a telephone report from Mother on the progress of the two ships. Apparently there was a slight panic when both vessels were delayed at Suez. A very patient and caring library staff explained to anxious relatives that the Canal could only take traffic one way at a time and the way had to be cleared before Mediterranean-bound ships could proceed northwards to Port Said. This, said Mother in her most forceful, dignified manner, was disgusting. Why should her son, after serving six long years for king and country, be suffering stupid delays in returning home to his loved ones?

The object of this concern was, meanwhile, thoroughly enjoying life. The war over there was no threat from aircraft, U-boats or surface raiders. Providing we did not run into any unswept mines safe passage was assured. In the relaxed atmosphere most of us, during the passage across the Indian Ocean and up the Red Sea slept on deck – one blanket and a pillow was all we needed. It also kept down the numbers of unwanted guests and considerably reduced the necessity to hunt, scratch and destroy. The two days delay at Suez were not, primarily, due to Canal traffic control reasons. We took on board an army unit whose speciality was delousing. Inspired by the hospitality of the crew and passengers this unit worked enthusiastically through the ship from keel to transom, as the saying goes. Not completely satisfied that all unloved passengers had been eliminated they stayed with us all the way up the canal to Port Said where we said a fond farewell with the sincere promise that next time we were lousy we would think of them first.

Leaving Port Said the difference in climatic conditions, although summer, was immediately noticeable. After the Indian Ocean, the Red Sea and Suez Canal the Mediterranean was relatively cool. Kit bags were hastily unearthed, shorts and bush shirts were replaced by the more familiar blue uniforms. Only the few hardy slept on deck at night, the rest of us swung contentedly below in our hammocks, insect-free and dreaming of the homecoming welcome awaiting us.

It was good to sail peacefully past Malta in brilliant sunshine. I could just make out to the south the faint outline of the Tunisian coast where three years before, I had been with the First Airborne Division prior to the invasion of Sicily. Three years had been a long time.

It was early morning at the beginning of June 1946 when the "Andes" docked in Southampton. There were no brass bands playing or cheering crowds to greet us. The war had been over a year and to some people we were already an embarrassment. Apparently the hope was that we would settle back into some civilian occupation without causing too much trouble. I'm not sure quite what we expected, but our high spirits were somewhat deflated as we disembarked off the "Andes" into the waiting troop train. The motherly smiles from the ladies from one of the voluntary organisations who came round the compartments distributing packed sandwiches did something to alleviate our blues. Their concern at their inability to provide us with any sort of liquid refreshment we alleviated by assuring them that during our many years in the forces we had become accustomed to such tribulations. We didn't tell them that most of us had at least three cans of beer in our haversacks.

Our destination was Kirkham, just outside Blackpool or, to be precise a camp at Warton on the banks of the River Ribble. Discipline at this camp was totally relaxed, providing one turned up at the appointed times at various venues for medical examinations. Not one inch of the human body was left untouched or un-probed. The standard of fitness for demobilisation, it seemed, was even higher than that required than that on enlistment, or so the male nurses with great glee informed us, so that a grateful government in years to come could refuse to pay war disability pensions as we were totally fit on discharge – and they could prove it. I'm sure that wasn't true, but it was a favourite topic of debate in the local pubs at night.

The telephone kiosks outside the camp and in the village were extremely busy and had long queues as men rang home to inform their loved ones of their safe arrival back in the United Kingdom. I found myself curiously tongue-tied when speaking to Nora, my wife. After a long separation we had so much to talk about that neither of us knew what to say. Mother was different, demanding to know why I was not home but "playing about in Blackpool" for a week after I had landed at Southampton. There was a threat that Winston Churchill would be hearing about it if there wasn't action soon.

The demobilisation process, however, took its course and it was another three days when, together with about thirty others, I was taken to a large hangar, given a cardboard box, and told to equip myself for civilian life. After collecting two sets of underpants, vests socks and shirts came the dilemma of selecting a suit. There were so many to chooses from that we milled about in total confusion. The problem was solved when a small corporal with a big voice picked me out from the mob as an example to the rest. "Apart from the obvious, and we don't want to know about your sex life, what are you going to do when you leave this exotic existence and enter civvy street? Assuming you change this life of overpaid idleness and you are going to work for a living. What at – are you going to be a parson, a bookie, a bricklayer or a pimp?" On hearing my muttered reply, "a railway clerk," he reached behind him, pulled out a suit and thrust it at me. "Here you are then, the right size and style as well. Who's next?" That man was a genius, the size was right – more or less – and the style certainly better than that of the tie I selected to go along with it. I was never allowed to wear that until many years later in a Boy Scout Gang Show comedy sketch. A raincoat and trilby hat completed my civilian ensemble. Like the tie the hat was a disaster, its second public appearance was as the Guy's crowning glory one Bonfire night.

The following day I was given a railway voucher, money for a month's leave and food ration coupons. I had decided to go home in uniform, my new civilian clothing felt strange and awkward. Struggling across Manchester from Victoria station to London Road (now Piccadilly) station with my cardboard box of civilian clothes in one hand and a kitbag containing my remaining RAF equipment and personal treasures slung over one shoulder I felt myself becoming increasingly nervous. Previously when coming home on leave, I had been excited and looking forward to some days of pleasure. This was very different. After six years I was coming home for good, and I was about to begin a new kind of life.........

There would be no going back to the comradeship of the Air Force which, I had only just realised, had been rich in experience and emotion. It had been a long time. At least I had survived. Many of my friends had died, there would be no family reunion for them. I wondered why I had been so lucky. These were strange thoughts walking past the bomb-damaged buildings of the city centre and as I boarded the train for the final leg of the journey home.

Alighting at Poynton, my village station, the feeling of unrealism increased. It had been ten years since I had left school and started work here. It seemed more like a century ago. Nothing had changed, except the people. I did not recognise one face – and no one knew me either – or so I thought.

It was a lovely summer's evening as I slowly walked the last mile and, as I turned the corner by the church lych-gate standing in front of our home across the road, I saw the slight figure of my wife Nora, holding the hand of a little boy – my son Bryan, aged three. I had been identified after all, and my arrival duly reported.

All my inhibitions melted in the warmth of her greeting. My son, however, was more restrained in his welcome of this stranger receiving so much love and affection from his mother. During his short life he had been the only male in the household and it was natural to resent what he saw as an intrusion on his so-far ordered life. He resisted all attempts to say "welcome home Dada" but, after suffering an hour during which my mother, mother-in-law and neighbours made a great fuss, came and stood gravely before me. He was obviously going to say something, and in the expectant hush he did.

"Go back to Bombay."

Well, I didn't and now, over fifty years later our relationship has improved to the point when I can say we even like each other.

Despite my fears life has been kind to me. I had a good marriage to a wonderful girl. Sadly I was to lose her after nearly forty years, but have been incredibly fortunate in finding a second partner who, although different in many ways, is equally as good to me.

I am grateful for life and what it has given me.

I have been lucky.